More **Praise for Char**

Charlotte's advice and insights
tion from Big 4 consulting to
Mouse is not only pragmatic, pr........, ...
ing read. I view it as required reading for anyone looking at a career transition,
whether now or in the future.

—Gary Siegel, Former Accenture partner

Charlotte Lee provides actionable ideas that keep you focused on what's really
important in finding your dream job. She combines compelling insights and
practical experience to help people stay motivated and keep focused on finding
that perfect job. This book is a valuable addition to self-improvement literature.

—Kim Pascale, WPP, Inc.

Maybe you can't find a job because you're doing or saying the wrong things.
Charlotte helps people identify and address their shortcomings and provides
excellent strategic advice. Working with her helped me transition to a new career
path and has brightened my personal relationships as well.

—Kuni Chen, CFA, NatureVest

While most career guides are theoretical, Charlotte's provides the most practical
and actionable job-search techniques and was key to my successful transition
from Wall Street to the media industry!

—P. Sean Gupta, BET

Charlotte's intimate knowledge of the job market and keen sense of how to
navigate a difficult environment allowed me to make a mid-career transition at
a senior level. I'm now thriving in my new position, and, looking back, I see that
she played the central role in resurrecting my career. Thank you, Charlotte!

—Damian Valentino, MSCI Barra

Charlotte has guided hundreds of professionals through career changes, so you
are now holding many lifetimes' worth of valuable experience, distilled down to
a few pages. You'll find yourself picking up this book again and again, whether
you're looking to move companies or move within one.

—Michelle Pearl Tien, Credit Suisse

Powerful. Inspiring. Reassuring. Powerful because it provides a time-tested
game plan that allows you to "see around the corners" during your journey.
Inspiring because it lays out exactly what to do and when to do it. Reassuring because it provides you with answers before you even have questions. No
time for trial and error. Invest an hour or two today, and you'll save weeks—or
months—in the pursuit of your perfect job.

—Joe D'Agostino, WestEnd Advisors, LLC

Bring a Dead Mouse
The Secret to Finding Your Perfect Job

Completely Updated 3rd Edition

by Charlotte A. Lee

B.A.D. Mouse Publishing, Inc.
2017

For LHH, a company built on values to live by, and filled with executives who are making the world a better place.

ISBN Print: 978-0-9905353-3-1
ISBN ebook: 978-0-9905353-4-8

Printed in the United States of America

First Edition, February 2011
Second Edition, July 2014
Third Edition, September 2017

Design and Layout: Rick Soldin (book-comp.com)

www.BringADeadMouse.com

Contents

Notes

A Brief—But Important—Note:
What's the Deal
with Dead Mice?

My mom, Gloria Lee, and one of her favorite cats.

The phrases "bring a dead mouse" and "finding a job" aren't typically found in the same paragraph, and I'm pretty sure they've never been seen side by side in the title of a book. But hang in there with me for a minute and I'll explain.

My mom used to tell me that when she was growing up in Charlotte, North Carolina, the family's pet cats would occasionally drop dead mice at her feet when she stepped out of her door to go to school. At first, she was disgusted (who wouldn't be?). But she eventually realized that those mice were actually presents, the cats' special way of showing her they were thinking of her. Yuck.

But my mom (or was it the cats?) had a point. One of the most powerful techniques you can use in your job search is to make yourself memorable. And one of the most powerful ways of making yourself memorable is to bring small "gifts" to the people you're meeting with. Later on in this book, we'll talk more about how to select the best dead mouse. But let me leave you with a phrase that every client I've ever worked with has heard me say at least once: "Memorable is hireable." And that's what this book is all about.

In addition, sometimes you're in a role and just not happy, or you don't think it's using all of your skills or going anywhere. This book and some of the tips and techniques can help you manage your professional growth, explore a new industry, or help you get engaged again. According to Gallup's recent reports on the American workplace, 68% of U.S. employees are either "not engaged" or "actively disengaged" at work. And a recent Harris survey found that 59% of working adults—and 73% of those in their 30s—want to change careers. If this is you, read on!

Preface

The journey to finding the right job is a world unto itself, particularly for those of us who believe that if we simply use the approaches that have brought us success in the workplace, things will continue to fall into place and bring us success in the future. Unfortunately, finding and transitioning to a wonderful new job has its own set of secret guidelines. But once you learn Charlotte Lee's key concepts, you'll be well on your way.

Charlotte has an intuitive, almost uncanny grasp of the rules for success in the mysterious world of job hunting, and I am very fortunate to have received personal coaching from her. At the beginning, it took me a while to fully embrace both the spirit and letter of her guidance. However, once I fully embraced her approach—which I encourage you to do as quickly as possible—I felt as if I had a magic wand.

Charlotte herself is strong, warm, direct, and inspirational. And all of this comes through in this short but compelling book on how to successfully get your dream job. Each chapter covers an important aspect of the job-search process. She uses simple, clear language to communicate why each component is important and what you need to do to implement it. It's a recipe for a wonderful outcome, so follow it carefully.

Jolie Eisner
East West Bank

Notes

Introduction

Why This Book?

Every morning, on my way to work, I walk past the New York Public Library, the building flanked by two enormous lions, Patience and Fortitude. And every morning I'm reminded that searching for a job—particularly in this economy—takes exactly those two qualities: patience and fortitude.

Statistics about how long it takes to find a job are all over the place and depend on a number of factors, including the type of job you're looking for, how long you've been out of work, and your age. But based on my experience working with thousands of clients, I can give you some pretty solid estimates: If you're looking for an executive job, expect to spend at least 10 months. If you're unemployed, plan on around six months if you're under 40, nearly twice that if you're over 50. And the longer you've been out of work, the longer it'll take. You'll need a lot of patience and fortitude to keep focused on your search for that amount of time. And you'll need it to cope with the warped sense of time that job hunting creates.

There are two time zones: one for those who are working and one for those out of work. It goes like this: You send an email to a hiring manager and expect a timely response. But your definition of timely and the manager's probably aren't the same. For you, 24 hours seems about right. Maybe 48. Any more than that will seem like foreeeeever. But for the manager, a week might be rushing it. Remember, they have full-time jobs, families, and other important obligations. And they probably get more than 100 emails every day. So take a deep breath and try to relax. It can sometimes take as many as seven attempts before you actually make contact with the person you're trying to reach. A job search is a marathon, not a sprint.

Remember when you were working full-time? You may not have been as responsive to every call and email as you should have, so try to be patient. Sometimes it's really not about you. I remember speaking with a client who mentioned that he had never responded to recruiters' or headhunters' calls. But now, he was annoyed at their unresponsiveness towards him! What goes around, comes around, I'm afraid.

Being unemployed or underemployed—especially if it lasts the better part of a year—can be extremely demoralizing. The Great Recession that began in 2007-08 (and continues to this day) has created perhaps the most difficult job market in decades. To start with, our economy is still on somewhat shaky ground. Plus, there are fewer large companies and more niche players.

Although the official unemployment rate has been dropping steadily, there are 15 million more Americans out of the labor force today (meaning that they've been out of work so long that they gave up and are no longer counted as unemployed) than there were a decade ago (about 80 million vs. 95 million).

And the competition for jobs in today's market is fiercer than ever. The good old days when all you had to do to get a job was match up the skills on your resume to an online job spec are long gone. And they're not coming back anytime soon. In addition, when I surveyed nearly 100 of my last clients, only one is working for an old boss from 20 years ago. That means your new boss/hiring manager will probably be a stranger to you, not a friend or family member. That's why you have to get outside your network and meet with your network's network and venture out further afield than ever.

Today, human resources experts tell me that they hire fewer than five percent of applicants. And why not? Hiring is now a buyers' market. The applicant pool is well stocked with highly qualified people with powerful skills and impressive CVs. Not surprisingly, employers have raised their expectations for applicants. Hiring managers tend to be conservative, holding out for candidates clearly able to do the job—usually candidates who've already done the job successfully elsewhere. In the new paradigm, you need to establish your value in the marketplace. To do that, you need to listen actively to potential employers about what's keeping them up at night. Then you need to figure out which of your skills will fix their problem and how you're going to persuade them to hire you as either a contractor or a full-time employee. You've got to show them you can help them meet the challenges they face, simply and seamlessly.

The path between you and your next job is a numbers game, pure and simple, and she or he with the most face-to-face meetings wins. Why? First, because face-to-face interviews give you valuable practice, and by the time you get to the hiring manager, you're a rock star. Second, because the more people you speak with, the better the chance that you'll hit on one who has a problem you can help solve. You can shape your job search and its outcome by how you choose to approach it, focusing on the approach that will most increase your likelihood of success. The more people you know within an organization, the better your campaign to work there will be. The trick is to get those people to start creating some buzz about you.

There are two sure-fire ways to sink your search. First, be alone. Second, be online more than two hours per day. Instead, go out and meet some people, because people hire people. No one's going to hire you based on an online resume or a phone call. You'll get hired only after someone meets you in person and discovers that you have both the skills and the personality to be successful in their firm. Not convinced by how important face-to-face meetings are? Consider this: According to the 2017 Job Outlook Survey by the National Association of Colleges and Employers, the top five skills employers want from their new hires are ability to work as a team, problem-solving skills, written communication skills, strong work ethic, and verbal communication skills—all of which can be assessed only in person.

The biggest predictor of job-hunting success? Optimism. Staying positive, keeping your chin up, and your energy and expectations high will take all the fortitude you can muster. Finding that optimism within yourself will allow you to go out into the world, connect with the right people, and find the job you want and deserve. One common thread that can be pulled through so many successful job landings is the high likeability factor. And happy people are a lot more likeable.

So how do I know all this, and what qualifies me to write a book on job hunting? Well, I'm a senior vice president with Lee Hecht Harrison, the largest outplacement firm in the world, with 300 offices in 67 countries. In this role, I coach senior executives in a variety of industries, including legal, financial, consumer, telecom, media, pharma, and professional services. Perhaps more important than any of that, I'm a career coach with a winning record. Ninety-eight percent of my clients have found jobs. Ninety-eight percent. In fact, I've been doing this for so long—and so successfully—that many of my old clients are hiring my new ones!

There's no shortage of job-search books, websites, and other resources out there. And there's no question that some of them can be quite helpful. However, times have changed since even the best of them were written. According to the U.S. Department of Labor Statistics, the average person will have 12 jobs between the ages of 18 and 48. For Millennials, that number could be as high as 15 (seven of which by age 28). Some of those job changes will be voluntary, others not so much.

The job-hunting landscape—the buyers' market paradigm—isn't going to change anytime soon. I believe that what people really need these days are solid, practical job-search ideas and approaches. In other words, a real "how to" rather than a "what" or "why" kind of book. And that's exactly what you're going to get in these pages. You'll hear from real, formerly out-of-work professionals how they found new roles and successfully transitioned back to work. And you'll get the specific tools and strategies you can use to land your next job—regardless of where you're located or what industry you're targeting.

The book is divided into 12 chapters, each one with a clear message and strategies that are designed to get you closer to your ultimate goal. Two of those chapters (one on negotiation dos and don'ts, the other on special situations, including returning to the workplace after military service and searching for work after long-term unemployment) are completely new to this book. There's also a very important FAQ section (with answers, of course). But all told, this small book is greater than the sum of its chapters. I know it's tempting to skip around, but try to go through the book in order. You'll be a lot happier with the results.

A couple of last-minute thoughts which you'll read more about in the coming pages. Every day, you have to be the solution to a business problem faced by a prospective employer. Make sure your generosity shines through. Sometimes it's just a kind word, quick email or phone call, a card dropped in the mail randomly, or a text that took you three seconds to send. Whatever it is, do it. You're creating positive karma around yourself and people will remember you well. If you do one a day, that's 365 positive items out there in the Universe about you. Wow! My client Maryanne had so much positive karma out there that very few of her emails went unanswered.

Your Career Mechanic

As we go through this book, I want you to think of your career as a vintage car that you want to restore, and of me as a trusted, full-service mechanic who's going to help you get that car back into tip-top shape. And don't worry; I'm not going to try to sell you a bunch of stuff that you don't need.

When you arrive at the garage, I can see that the car is running a little rough—otherwise, you wouldn't be there, right? So the first thing I'm going to do is pop the hood to see what's happening. When I do that with my clients, I find that some of them need only a few relatively minor things. For example, you might need:

◊ A tune-up. A basic resume tweak, to make sure you're using the best format, the best wording, and are presenting yourself in the best possible way.

◊ Fuel-ignition/spark plugs. Sometimes what's keeping you from getting where you want to go is a problem of energy. Are you passive and reserved or upbeat and positive? You don't need to be the Energizer Bunny, but you do need to come across as engaged and interested.

◊ Radiator light is on. If you've been in the same job or field for a long time, you may have lost some of your passion, which has put you in danger of burning out. We'll have to figure out whether the problem is normal wear and tear that can be solved by topping off your antifreeze and water, or whether you've got a leak. And if it's a leak, is it repairable or are you going to need a completely new radiator?

◊ Flat tire. Flat tires make for a bumpy ride. We need to make sure that when you're explaining your value proposition and what you can do for a prospective employer, you're smooth and pitch-perfect. But you don't want to put too much air in. Over-inflated tires (and egos) can cause problems.

Sometimes a client comes in with a car that has more serious issues. For example:

◊ It's not running at all. In cases like that, we need to take a look at every one of the vehicle's systems to figure out what's causing the problem. We'll do that over the course of this book.

◊ GPS problems. A lot of clients spend time and money on a job search, but they really don't know what it is that they want to do. As New York Yankees' great Yogi Berra said, "If you don't know where you're going, you might not get there." So let's make sure your GPS maps are updated so we can get you pointed in the right direction.

Before I let clients leave my garage, I always evaluate their vehicle for cosmetic issues, including their paint job and upholstery. We all know that we shouldn't evaluate books by their covers, that beauty comes from within, and that people should see us for who we are, not what we look like. But we do it anyway. You'll have a much easier time selling a shiny, beautiful-looking car that runs like crap than a filthy, dented one that runs beautifully. In fact, most people won't even bother to test-drive the ugly one. Same goes for your job search. Seemingly superficial things count. A lot. We'll talk more about this in Chapter 4.

Now, let's get started!

Chapter 1

Know—and Differentiate—Thyself

If you're ever going to have even the slimmest chance of standing out in a crowded marketplace, it's essential that you have a solid understanding of who you are, what you do well, and how to brand and differentiate yourself.

On the most basic level, differentiation is your ability to be memorable. And memorable is hireable. Think about it this way: After you've had your interviews and walked out of the room, what will people remember? They'll remember that the procurement guy was a former Navy SEAL, that the banker with the blond hair is fluent in Mandarin, that Roger was a Rhodes Scholar, Aisha is a designer (but a lawyer by training), Rob is an Eagle Scout, Karen is an MBA, CFA, and CPA, and Pamela is a Master Black Belt in Six Sigma. These are all great differentiators—making these candidates unique and stand out from the crowd. And that's a good thing, given that, as I've mentioned, this is a buyers' market, where employers can get exactly whom and what they want in an employee.

So what will people remember about you?

The things that make you memorable—the things that make you uniquely "you"—are your brand, and you want to make sure you've got two of them: a professional one and a personal one. They should be different from each other, but should each reflect a skill or something unique about you that the company you're interviewing needs. Chris's Air Force background and his service as an intelligence officer in Iraq was a great conversation starter and definitely differentiated him from most other candidates.

One important thing to remember about brands—personal as well as professional—is that they respond to a need—they rarely ever create a need. Think Mercedes versus Porsche; Harvard versus Princeton; Goldman Sachs versus Bank of America. Each one of those brands—and that's exactly what they are—is built around responding to the needs of a particular segment of the larger marketplace. Let me give you another example. Toyota has a very strong brand, but they recognized that most people looking to buy a luxury car would drive right past the Toyota dealership. So they created Lexus, a purely luxury brand. Similarly, hip, young car buyers would also have driven right past the Toyota dealership—after all, Toyota was their parents' car company. So Toyota created Scion. (Interestingly, in 2016, Toyota's research found that the current generation of young car buyers isn't quite as worried about standing out from their parents and is, in fact, buying Toyotas because they're reliable. So the company pulled the plug on Scion.)

Toyota clearly understands its brands—including their potential and their limitations—extremely well and reacts accordingly. Before you can find your next job, you're going to have to develop a thorough grasp of your own personal brand. What specific need is your brand responding to and how are you uniquely qualified to satisfy it? (In marketing terms, what's your value proposition or unique selling proposition?) This isn't a step you can take lightly or skip over. In my view, it's the foundation for everything you'll ever do in your career, and the most difficult part of the job-search process. It's how you articulate who you are, and how you can present the value-add that you bring to any potential employer.

Your personal brand is made up of three distinct components, which, together, I call your inventory:

◊ Your skill sets

◊ Your operating style

◊ Your personal style

Let's take a look at each one in a bit more detail.

Your skill sets are pretty easy to identify. Are you a CPA, FP&A, COO, CEO, CFA, operations expert, IT guru, project manager, etc.? My lovely client Elaine has 11 certifications.

She's a knowledge expert with very impressive credentials in the increasingly important, and highly technical field of information management. Those certifications get that message across. Mitch got his FMR on his own, and Andrea picked up that AML certificate. Kamilla is working towards her CPA, and Marcus is earning his MBA at night. But whether you have initials after your name or you've earned some kind of official certification, the process is the same: Come up with a detailed list of everything you actually do—all of your skills. Do you manage people, analyze data, reduce costs, streamline processes, generate revenues, develop strategies, or market products? Great—write it down. And don't limit yourself to my list. This process is about you, so think about all of your skills—even the ones that you may not think are business-related. One of Jeff's best skills was mentoring junior professionals at the firm. And Michael is especially adept at explaining complex financial structures in such a way that even non-finance people can easily understand them. Know your strengths and weaknesses and be able to articulate them clearly and simply with impact.

Your operating style is a description of the way you work. Ask yourself these questions (and get a good handle on the answers, since you'll probably get asked many of the same ones in job interviews!): Are you collaborative or dictatorial? Do you work better alone or on a team? How do others perceive you—whether they're junior or senior to you? What would your last boss say about you? How would they describe the way you work? What do you think you're known for? Are you the go-to person or an impediment to the process? Part of the solution or part of the problem? In this job market (and any other time, for that matter), you must come to the table with solutions. You need to be a problem solver.

If you've never been assessed or gone through a 360 evaluation, consider completing a Myers-Briggs Type Indicator assessment, which you can find free online here: https://www.mbtionline.com/. Also ask others for feedback and be open to it. Just take it in; don't say anything, get defensive, or get upset or they'll stop speaking. Remember, your eyes and body language give away your emotions, so control your fidgeting, smile, and lean forward—no arms crossed and no furrowed brow. Most of us aren't as self-aware as we think we are. One day I was speaking with my deputy, Ro, and said, "Isn't it great that my office door is open and that I'm using Jack Welch's Management by Walking Around style and casually chatting with folks?" Ro laughed and said, "When people see your door open and hear you coming out, they run! They're petrified of you!" I was stunned. It was clearly time to slow down, smile more, ask more questions, and soften my approach! That's something I work on every single day!

Your personal style is a deceptively simple component of your brand, but you'll have a terrible time finding a job if you can't identify it. Are you formal or informal? Conservative or liberal? Extroverted or introverted? The life of the party or a wallflower? Picture a bright light and a bunch of moths moving towards it. Are you the light or the moth? Do people move towards you or are you the one who moves?

In the old human resources adage, "Can do, will do, fit," this is the fit part. We're in a buyers' market, and everyone out there has the skills ("can do") and desire ("will do") to do the job. So it all comes down to fit. Employers are looking for soft skills that may give them a hint as to whether you'll work well with the rest of the team and whether you'll successfully leverage the company's brand/product and grow their business. These are intangible skills that have very little to do with your core competencies, but are just as important. Do you make eye contact when you speak to people? Do you communicate well? How's your body language—do you come across as meek, aggressive, angry, confident? Do you seem like more of a leader or a follower?

No one has the time or the patience to deal with prima donnas, high-maintenance employees, or difficult personalities. The Great Recession and the painfully slow recovery in its wake has provided the perfect cover for employers looking to get rid of employees who just don't fit.

The current market calls for a lot of flexibility on the job seeker's part. Of course, you want to be authentic, but you also have to build excellent rapport with everyone you interview with. These days, when most hiring is done by consensus, you may need to get more than a dozen people to like you and want you on board. Modify your behavior to fit with the person you're meeting with. It's not enough to know what you did, do, or want. You need to evaluate your audience, learn what they need, and move to it. That includes the receptionist and the assistant. One of my clients, Mike, once started a networking conversation with someone, and ended up with a job. When they told him what their challenge was, Mike responded with a solution he had implemented in a previous role—and it worked!

Have the same level of respect for each person. You don't want to be seen as elitist, so treat everyone the same.

You never know how any one person's opinion will impact the decision to hire you—or not.

Overall, your brand should reflect a distinctive combination of skill sets or something unique about you that your prospective employer needs. Unfortunately, it's often hard to predict what that's going to be. Many people who meet me remember that I was president of Habitat for Humanity in Nassau County, and not someone who used to work for investment banking firms. Go figure. You just don't know what will stand out. But as long as you do stand out, it's okay. Remember to trot out a few things in case the one you love doesn't resonate with your audience. You never know what's going to click, but if you do your research, you'll hit pay dirt.

As a personal branding exercise, I recommend that you spend some time creating a branding word cloud that lists your skill sets and the characteristics that make you the unique candidate you are. Below you'll find one I did for myself. If you've got a piece of software that will let you design a word cloud, great (if you don't, just Google "word cloud generator"), but you can also do it the old-fashioned way, with pencil (because you'll do a few dozen versions before you get it right) and paper. By the way, your word cloud is just for you and anyone else you want to get help from—you're not going to give it to anyone you're interviewing or networking with. Oh, and speaking of words, you might also want to check out Jobscan (jobscan.co), which analyzes job descriptions and optimizes your resume by suggesting word changes that will make your resume better resonate with recruiters.

Trusted
Passionate *Mentor*
Advisor Confidence Builder
Transferability C-Suite
Skillset **Coach** *Dynamic*
Integrity Authentecity Leader
Brand Improvement Energy
Strategies
Presence
Network

Once you've spent some time considering the three facets of your inventory and putting everything down on paper (or digitally), it's time to start mapping out your plan of attack.

Key Takeaways

- ♦ You must have a solid understanding of who you are, what you do well, and how to differentiate yourself.
- ♦ Brands—including your personal one—respond to a need; they rarely ever create one.
- ♦ Your brand is made up of three distinct components: your skill set, your operating style, and your personal style.
- ♦ It's all about "fit." In a buyers' market, everyone has the skills to do the job. But not everyone will mesh well with the hiring company's style and culture.

Chapter 2

Embracing Risk: Courage as a Skill Set

Finding a job is one of the hardest things you'll ever do. Harder than getting married, harder than having a baby, and even harder than raising a child. Why is job hunting so difficult? In my view, the two biggest reasons are (1) you'll need to take risks—something most people dread, and (2) it requires asking for help—something very few people feel comfortable doing (more on that below). Fortunately, both of these skills are easily learned.

Let's start with taking risks. Actually, let's talk about complacency, which is the opposite of taking risks. Complacency often feels pretty comfortable and may even make you feel secure in your current situation. So what does complacency look like? Well, it's when you keep on doing things the way you've always done them, and you never do anything to make yourself memorable or invaluable. So if you arrive and leave at the same time every day, wear the same type of outfits, eat lunch at the same time and with the same people, and you don't volunteer for new projects, organize the Holiday party, get to know the new hires, or go out of your way to impress your boss, you're being complacent. And the big problem with complacency is that it never lasts. If you're complacent in your job, you won't be there for long. If you're complacent in your job search, you're going to be out of work a lot longer than necessary.

Think about it this way: When you're employed, you're taking frequent, small risks over a long period of time. When you're out of work, you need to take less-frequent, larger risks over a shorter period of time.

Taking risks in your job search means getting out of your comfort zone and doing things a little (or a lot) differently. When was the last time you had a great idea—and actually shared it with other people? Have you ever spoken up in a job forum to ask a question? Have you taken the initiative and offered to mentor a junior person, or asked a senior person out to lunch? Have you organized a community service day or event for your firm? Have you introduced yourself to the new guy—and everyone else on your floor?

The key to getting out of your comfort zone is to take small steps. With each step, that zone gets a little bigger and a little wider, and the more you do, the more you'll find you can do. Take a small step today! You'll be moving in a wider zone tomorrow.

Every time you speak to a stranger, call up a colleague you haven't seen in years, or send a LinkedIn invite to someone you barely know, you're taking a risk.

There's no question that rejection can sting. But, really and truly, what's the worst they can do? Ignore you or say "No." So what? As my mother-in-law often said, "It's not a train wreck!" No harm, no foul, so just move on. At least 80 percent of the time, it's not personal—they don't hate you. It's just that they don't have (or can't make) the time right now; everyone's being asked to do more with less. Suffering this kind of rejection—and learning that the world hasn't come to an end—will actually strengthen you and give you the courage you'll need to take more—and bigger—risks in the future. So, rather than take the rejection personally, just move on.

Now that you've got a handle on risk-taking, let's talk about something that may scare more people than the possibility of rejection: asking for help. Asking for help can be a pretty frightening thing to contemplate, let alone do. But here's the way you need to look at it: If your dishwasher broke, your kitchen is flooded, and you don't know how to fix it, you're going to call a plumber. Or if you've been on a particular diet for a few months and your weight isn't changing, you should probably call Weight Watchers. There's a lot of stuff we can't do by ourselves. And it's a far better use of our time and resources to find someone who can truly help than try to muddle through things on our own.

The most effective way to reduce the scariness of asking for help is to consciously start helping other people as much as you can. It's a little like being the Godfather. You do favors and perform services for people all the time. It could be as small as making an introduction for them, or being a reference, or carpooling a day or two per week. Then, one day, when you need something, you can ask for it without feeling like a leech or a loser. In a sense, you're not actually asking for anything—it's almost as if you're collecting on a debt. (And the truth is that most people really do want to help you—they're just waiting to be asked.) So, from now on, make the business of helping others a priority in your life. Our society is built on reciprocity. We've all heard the old adage, "One hand washes the other." You go first, and others will follow your lead. And remember: when you land in your new job, pay it forward. What goes around really does come around.

Unfortunately, not everyone grasps that simple concept. I had a friend who broke her back. Every week for almost a year, I drove over to her house with a home-cooked meal and went for a walk with her—a little further each time. Not long after that, I had surgery and was homebound for a few months. This woman sent flowers but never came to visit or even called. In fact, I've never seen her again. But that hasn't kept me from doing the right thing whenever I can. Kindness is always a nice thing to extend, even when it's not reciprocated. It'll come back to you eventually.

If you happen to be out of work, take a quick look at Chapter 6, on dead mice, and start coming up with some dead mice of your own. This is a world of reciprocity and if you don't give, you won't get—and perhaps you shouldn't. Sometimes people just need a how're-you-doing email, or a little help with a networking issue, or an idea at work, or an article on something that fits their world. You want to have been leaving lots of dead mice on everyone's doorsteps all year round, so when it's your turn to ask for something, it won't seem strained. If you're trying to get a meeting with a specific person, track down some information you know he or she would find particularly interesting. It could be an article about something he personally or professionally cares about. Or some news about a person she knows. Maybe her child needs help with college essays and you're a terrific writer. Or maybe his wife is sick and you can deliver chicken soup to the house. Or a spouse is out of work and you can help him line up some networking meetings at your former company. You get the point.

I strongly suggest that you incorporate doing things for others into your daily life before you're in a situation when you need something from others. A lot of job hunters frantically reach out to all their LinkedIn contacts, former friends from college and previous jobs, and random people they met at cocktail parties. But I can tell you from experience (and from hearing the same things from many people I know) that it's often annoying to open up an email from someone I haven't heard from in five or 10 years (or longer) who wants me to do something for them.

Looking for a job is an activity that takes a ton of resilience and patience. You'll hear, "No, I can't see you," "No, I don't know anyone you can speak with," and "No, you didn't get the job." Over and over and over, for months on end. After every one of these knock-downs, you're going to have to pick yourself up, brush yourself off, and start all over again. You'll end up kissing a lot of frogs to get that prince or princess. But all it takes is one. My client Sara had 167 meetings, but only one got her the job. But since neither you nor I know which meeting will finally pay off, we have to do a great job with every one of them. Please consider rescheduling a meeting if you don't think you're able to bring your A game.

You have the talent, the knowledge, and the experience. All you need to do now is hang in there until you accomplish your goal. It's only one job—you can do it!

As you do all of this, it's important to keep your expectations reasonable. My client Peter was a C-suite executive for many years before losing his job. One afternoon, he came to my office and joined a group of 20 other out-of-work clients. Frustrated and angry, he slammed his hand on the conference table and said, "Dammit, I'm a senior guy and I expect people to call me back." Then, with eyes boring into the faces of all the startled candidates, he rather sheepishly added, "Boy, did I have to get over that pretty quickly." It would be great if everyone returned your calls and offered to do things for you (in the same way that you're selflessly doing things for others). But don't hold your breath. Sad, but true.

Many people find that their immediate network is actually a lot less helpful than they expected, and that, instead, it's the random acts of kindness from strangers (or a friend, or a friend of a friend) that make the difference. Always ask the person you're meeting with or speaking with whether there's anyone else they might be able to connect you with. Name a company or two to make it easier for people to help you. Or name a specific function ("Do you know any lawyers/real estate people/people in not-for-profits?").

It's time to leave that ego at the door and start asking for—and accepting—help. This is going to take some courage, as the person you're asking could ignore you or reject you, right? Go for it anyway! It's hard—especially if you've been rejected before—but take this tiny chance on humanity and I promise, you'll be pleasantly surprised. After all, if someone were to ask you for help, you'd honestly try, right? There are people out there who are in a position to do something for you, but in most cases, they won't offer unless you come right out and ask. Sometimes, that's simply because they don't know you need any help, or they don't know exactly how to help. You're going to have to come up with creative ways to ask, follow up, ask again, and thank them. Most importantly, when you do get that great job (and I know you will), please remember to pay it forward—in other words, do something for someone else before they ask you.

If you're in a job where you're not happy, consider taking the time to use LinkedIn to reconnect with long-lost friends, bosses, and colleagues—not just people you know from your most recent job. Spruce up your LinkedIn profile with an updated photo and your latest news. Send out a "Have a great week. Would love to reconnect" LinkedIn message with your contact info and see if anyone comes back to you—voila! Some catch-up meetings will now transpire. Call a friend (don't email...) who works for a company you admire. Ask good questions; see him/her for coffee. Email four or five people this month to "check in" and see how they're doing. Start making these outreaches now, when you don't need anything and can just listen to them vent, etc.

In your existing role, think of ways to improve your situation. Could you benefit from more communication with your peers, boss, or other departments? Should you be asking to be on more assignments, different, more interesting projects where you can sharpen or expand your skills? Is there a conference you'd like to attend where you could represent the firm? Is there one where you should be a speaker or panelist? Can you or should you volunteer just so you can be seen and see others? It's on you to start making your job better by opening and improving your communications. Remember, you can't change others, only yourself. Walk over to someone today and start improving your day-to-day job.

Twenty seconds of courage. That's all you need to send that email, make that call, ask that ask, meet that person, go through that door. It's never going to be completely easy, but the more you do it, the better and more empowered you'll feel, and the more progress you'll make in the search and in life. Life is about risks, and this one will take you only 20 seconds. That's it. Come on! You can do it!

Celebrate Every Win

Searching for a job is tough. It can also be frustrating, infuriating, and demoralizing, which is exactly why it's important to celebrate the milestones along the way. For example, Bruce finally emailed you back; Katherine returned your call; and you're having coffee with Tristan tomorrow. Sure, these are small victories and not all of them will lead to anything, but you wouldn't be able to land a job without them and many other small steps. So celebrate! When you're out of work, it's natural to focus on the end goal of landing a great job. But the journey is important too. Acknowledge the progress you're making, enjoy the wonderful people you'll meet along the way, and smell the roses every chance you get!

Key Takeaways

♦ Get used to taking risks. And stay as far away from complacency as possible.

♦ Get comfortable with asking for help—and accepting help. People won't offer if you don't ask. And helping others—especially when you don't need or want anything in return—always makes it easier for you to ask for their help later.

♦ Celebrate every win. Job search is tough and giving yourself a pat on the back for small achievements may help keep you focused and energized.

Notes

Chapter 3

Tools of the Trade

Most job seekers spend a lot of time writing, formatting, and polishing their resume. But, while there's no question that resumes are important, they're just one of the many tools you'll need if you're going to get the job you want with the employer you want to work with (but keep in mind that the average resume gets reviewed for four seconds. Yep, four whole seconds). Other essential tools of the job-search trade include your "elevator pitch" or positioning statement, your email address (more on that below), salary requirements, note cards (for old-fashioned thank-you notes), business cards, bullet points to high-light your strengths, and references. Additional tools are increasingly important as well. These include your LinkedIn profile, (Facebook too, depending upon your sector), a one-paragraph profile, a professional-quality headshot, a single phone number where you're reachable 24/7, a personalized URL, and an advisory board to keep you on track. Let's take a look at each of these tools in a little more detail.

Resume (or CV)

Two pages max, written in 10-point Arial or another easy-to-read, sans-serif font. Anything smaller than that is too hard to read—especially by people who pore over dozens of resumes every day. Hard-to-read resumes usually turn into unread resumes. Also, make sure your resume is in PDF format so that whenever you email it to anyone you can be confident that it'll look perfect when they open it.

Resume must-haves include: your full name, mailing address, email address, LinkedIn address, and cell phone number. In the Experience section, go back only 15 years. If you've been in the labor force longer than that, put in a section called Other Work Experience and just list the firm, your job title, and a one-line description. You don't need to list the specific years you were at each position in this section.

One resume must-have that most people overlook is ease of navigation. You're trying to draw people to the page, and an overly dense document with no white space is a turn-off. Remember, your resume is a marketing document, not a list of everything you've done for the past 25 years. Your ability to differentiate yourself in a crowded marketplace depends on your ability to clearly and concisely talk about your accomplishments.

Towards the end of the resume (the bottom of page 2), be sure to include an Additional Information section, which is for things about you that don't specifically fit anywhere else but make you an interesting candidate. For example, you've lived and worked in the US, Asia, and Europe; you speak French and Spanish; you founded an investment club for inner-city kids, and so on. My client Bob was an Eagle Scout, and I encouraged him to include it in the Additional Information section. He was amazed at how many times that came up in interviews and networking meetings.

The Additional Information section is also where you articulate how well you "fit" with the organization you're applying to (see Chapter 1 for more on this). Companies (and the individuals who work there) tend to hire people they like, who look a bit like them, who share similar values and interests. This section, while it may not seem terribly important, could give the person reading it a very valuable screening tool by providing some interesting "mutual interest" information. For example, if the hiring manager you're meeting with is big on mentoring, and you've been active with Big Brothers Big Sisters, you've just differentiated yourself from a whole bunch of other people—and formed a bit of a bond in the process. If the head of HR believes in public school education and you volunteer for Learning Leaders in the schools and became a Certified Literacy Tutor, you've just leapt ahead of your competition. So if you aren't already doing so, start thinking about causes that you believe in, and start giving back. It's great for the people you're helping, but helping others will make you feel great too. All it takes is a few hours a month. Give to Get.

Elevator Pitch and Verbal Positioning

One of the most important parts of any job search is getting the word out. Do not hide. Tell everyone you know that you're looking for your next great opportunity! That will force you to get your pitch down—nothing slows the wheels of progress more quickly than telling someone that you'll get back to them. You need to tell them right now. The elevator pitch is a quick, concise statement of who you are, what you've done, and what you want to do next. "I'm Sue Smith, a financial planning and analysis expert, most recently out of ABC company. They went through a major restructuring and eliminated my position, but it was a great place to work and I got some valuable experience there. Fortunately, my skills are fully transferable and I have excellent references, too." Your verbal positioning answers the question, "So why did you leave your last employer?" before they ask it. Usurping this question is a better approach.

Be sure to customize your elevator pitch for your audience and give specifics when appropriate. For example, if Sue is meeting with a CFO, she could say, "I've worked with three CFOs in my previous roles, and some of the items I prepared for them were... Might those be helpful to you?" With a bit of luck, this will pique that CFO's interest and she'll begin to brainstorm a bit with Sue—or at least give her some additional color on the role and the challenges the firm faces.

My client John has been using his elevator pitch to introduce himself to people during department meetings and one-on-one meetings with senior managers. Having practiced and refined it, he is able to present himself naturally and credibly to anyone anywhere. I often put clients in groups so we can practice (with strangers, as they usually don't know each other at first) and get constructive feedback on how they look and sound. Nothing warms my heart more than to hear one client tell another how much she/he has progressed from the first time they heard the pitch. Barbara told Laura, "Wow! You sound great now... Sooooo much better than last time!" Laura beamed, by the way. We all like an attaboy sometimes. Stu and John rarely smiled. Now that that's been brought to their attention, we discovered that they both had teeth and gums galore! Oh—and the room lights up when they smile.

Email Address

What we're doing here is reinforcing your branding, so try to include your actual name (joansmith@gmail.com—keep unicornmaster@fluffybunnies.com for your personal use). I recommend that you use Gmail (or, if you're fewer than five years out of school, your alumni.edu address is fine too). AOL screams "dated," and Hotmail and Yahoo! are close behind. Make sure the same email address appears on your resume, note cards, cover letters, and business cards. If you have more than one email account (and who doesn't these days?), be sure to set them up so they all forward to a single address.

Cover Letter

Short and sweet letters work best; three paragraphs is a good length. In the first paragraph, clearly say why you're writing, and be sure to include the title or type of job you're applying for. In the second paragraph, briefly talk about a few of the ways your skills and experience align perfectly with the job. Use some of the language in the job spec in your letter. Be sure to personalize it if at all possible. Think about ways you can be an extra pair of hands. What keeps them up at night? How can you help? And what differentiates you from the other candidates? In the third paragraph, you'll thank the person you're writing to for his or her time and consideration. If you're emailing your cover letter, make sure the letter itself is in the body of the email, not an attachment, and that you include only one link—the one that opens your resume. One click is all you get.

Salary Requirements

A lot of employers request this information because it allows them to screen out people who are asking for way too much, are too senior, or don't know what they're worth. If at all possible, try to get a salary range from the employer. You may be able to find that information on the company's website, job listings, a compensation website like glassdoor.com, or from someone you know who works there. If you can't find out the actual range, you'll have to come up with one of your own. A place to start is with the salary (not including any bonuses) that you earned at your previous job. If your earnings were all over the place, list an average for the past three years. In person or on the phone you can always turn a "what kind of salary are you expecting?" or "how much did you make last year?" question into "what's the range?" But unless you absolutely have to, do not include specific salary requirements in cover letters, on applications, or in any other written communication.

Note Cards

Note cards are for the handwritten thank-yous you're going to send to your centers of influence (people who have really gone above and beyond for you, or who might do so), as well as to accompany items you're sending to remind folks of who you are (all of this, of course, is in addition to the Thanksgiving or Holiday cards you usually send out). For example, a manager you met with spent some time talking about her recent trip to Versailles, and you follow up with an article you came across on the same topic. Sending something of interest to people you met recently is a wonderful way to keep your name fresh in their memory and remind them that you're still out there—without actually saying anything about yourself or asking for anything. This is a subtle, yet very powerful technique. Be sure the cards you buy are classic and lovely but not over the top. My client Elizabeth thought that the red print of her name, plus the red border on the card and the red lining of the envelope was too much, and just took the lining out. The cards were perfect then! Remember, less is more. Someone recently sent me a Christmas card, and inside the envelope was her husband's business card—he sells real estate… I don't recommend mixed messages.

Business Cards

Although people think of business cards as one of the first things you get after you start a job, I think they're also one of the first things to get when you *lose* your job. It's so much easier to ask for someone's business card if you're in the process of handing them yours. You don't want to start a conversation with, "I'm out of work," but you do want, by the end of the conversation, to know what the other person does and for him or her to know what you do and that you're looking for a new role. Everyone should have a business card. Whether you just got out of college, are hoping to retire soon, or anything in between, give out your cards and collect as many as you can from others.

Your cards should be printed on white or off-white, good-quality card stock. Yes, you may be able to take advantage of some of the "free" business cards some online printers offer, but stay far, far away if the price of "free" is putting an advertising message for the printer on the back of the card. In comes across as really cheap and unprofessional (plus, some people may use the back of your business card to jot down things they want to remember about you—where you met, what line of work you're in, and so on—and you want them to have as much room to write as possible). Ditto for wild colors or scents (yes, I've seen—and smelled—scented cards). If you're a designer or a marketing professional, you can do something unique to make your business cards stand out from the pile. A little color is okay—maybe a light blue line under your name, a red square above your name, or navy-blue ink instead of black. A little goes a long way, so nothing crazy. The more creative your field, the more color you can get away with. My client Victoria had her name in fuchsia with a fuchsia back on her card. It looked great and stood out in a good way. But this is about differentiating yourself, not making a political statement. Use the same color scheme, font, and logo if you use one (tasteful, original, not a piece of cute clip art you found on the Web) on all your printed materials.

Print the cards with the name people call you: Sandy Smith, not J.T. Sanford Lee Smith-Bell, VII. Since you're looking for work at this point and don't have an actual job title, list something like "Human Resources Executive" or "Finance Professional" under your name, if you wish. And always include professional credentials, such as CPA, SPHR, or ESQ, but skip educational ones (BA, BS or MBA). Make sure you customize your LinkedIn URL so that it ends with your name, not a bunch of random letters or numbers. Keep the design of the card very basic, something like this (note that the card does *not* include your address):

Charlize Weber, Esq.
General Counsel

(917) 555-5555

charlizeweber@gmail.com
linkedin.com/in/charlizeweber

Companies I have used in the past include Vistaprint, PrintPlace, Moo, and Morning Print.

Bullets

One of the biggest mistakes you can make at this stage of your job search is to use your resume as your calling card—especially for informational meetings. Once people see a resume, they immediately switch to "Oh-no-this-is-about-a-job" mode, and they're likely to brush you off with something designed to get you out of their office: "Sorry, we don't have a job like that," or, "I'll send it around," (which is code for "I'll send it to HR where they'll probably lose it under a pile of other unsolicited resumes," or, "I'll give it to Bob in accounting and you'll be his problem from now on."). That doesn't do much for you, but it makes the person who did it feel a little better about herself because she did something for you... Give your target people something about you so they can easily "pitch" you to someone else and introduce you without much trouble. Our job is to make it simple and easy for people to help us and introduce us to others.

Instead, craft a set of three bullet points to convey your brand—to highlight key aspects of who you are. These are short statements that describe you (for example: "12 years as an ABC exec," "CFO and Finance Director," "Colby College undergrad and Wharton MBA," "Operations manager with expertise in clearing and client account management."). When you're reaching out to introduce yourself to someone, remember to keep it short. When you're doing informational interviews, you're there to gather information, receive advice and guidance, learn about their business, and get to know a company's people and culture. So rather than pull out your resume, hand them your bullet points.

My client Rich chose to ignore this piece of advice, and insisted on leading with his resume. He talked about his background and his job search on every phone call and followed up with a resume. He was out of work—and barely had any meetings with anyone—for nine long months. Finally, he switched to bullets and almost immediately started landing face-to-face meetings.

You absolutely must get this right. Looking for a job is one of the hardest things you'll ever do. Trust me. I've done it more than a few times myself and I've coached thousands of clients through the process. Write your bullets out and have them at the ready in case someone says, "Send your resume over." If you hear that, you want to respond with something like this: "May I send some quick bullets instead? I know there are very few roles, and who has time to read a resume? If at all possible, I'd just love to get a short face-to-face meeting to introduce myself, get a little advice and perspective, and widen my network."

Examples of these bullets might be:

◊ Ex-ABC company for 8 years

◊ Ex-DEF company for 6 years

◊ Project manager and product specialist

◊ Bachelor of Science in Engineering, AAA University

◊ PMI Certified; Six Sigma Green Belt

Use your bullets to make it easier for you to set up 10-15-minute networking meetings and get advice, and for other people to introduce you to their network. Don't even mention a job—right now all we're doing is trying to open doors, widen our network, practice our elevator pitch, and build rapport. The easier you make it for people, the more likely they'll want to help you. Here's an example of the kind of email you'd like them to send on your behalf.

Subject: My friend Charlotte

Hi Steve,
Hope you're well and that the Jets have a better season next year! I was wondering if you would be willing to have a short networking meeting with my friend Charlotte? She was most recently with ABC company (more info below) and just wanted to get some advice about CDE company and you.

Thanks and best,
Laura
(444) 444-4444

References

Be sure you have three to six references from previous roles. Ideally, you'll have a diverse group so that each one can cover different territory. This will let prospective employers know that you can work with all kinds of people in all kinds of situations. Contact your references ahead of time to go over the points you want them to mention. After you speak with them on the phone, send a follow-up email thanking them for being your reference and reiterating what the two of you spoke about and what their sound bites are. Try not to use the same people over and over again. When providing reference lists to prospective employers, unless your reference says otherwise, include only his or her personal email address and cell phones rather than their work ones where there may be restrictions on what they may or may not say during their business day or on utilizing their firm's resources. When listing the reference, be sure to include some context so the person contacting the reference knows whether they're talking to a colleague, peer, manager, boss, or someone else.

More Essential Tools for Everyday Presentation

A LinkedIn profile. More and more headhunters are dispensing with their own databases and are using LinkedIn instead. Your LinkedIn profile should be at least 90 percent complete, include a photo (profiles with a headshot are viewed 17 times more often than those without), and mention 6–8 business-related groups that you're a member of. And think about the number of connections you have; those with 500 or more appear higher up in searches. Leave your most recent employer as "current" for 90 days after you've left. You'll also want to include several recommendations (but proof each of them yourself first before the person uploads it to your profile page). And, if anyone ever offers to write a recommendation for you, say Yes. One last word on recommendations: I've been known, when in doubt, to ask recommenders to use only their first name and last initial. That way, if that person is a polarizing figure in your marketplace, there won't be any negative spillover on you. My client Brandon said he could have an extremely senior person at a large investment banking firm give him a recommendation. Unfortunately, there are a lot of people who aren't crazy about that particular senior executive.

Melina is an over-50 client who didn't have a LinkedIn profile when she started her search. But by the time she left our practice and landed a job, she had more than 200 connections and a great photo up. Do not underestimate the importance of this online tool! If you're not already on there, get on, get a pic up, and get started making connections! Five hundred connections is a good number to shoot for.

Bio. This is something you'll need to come up with anyway, if you're planning to do consulting or give speeches. Your bio should be in prose. No poetry, no iambic pentameter, no bullets. Include the same photo that's on your LinkedIn profile.

Photo. Photos are important, so upload a couple of good headshots of you in professional clothing to your Facebook page. The photo should be in color, and you should be smiling and wearing business or business/casual clothes. Have a nice haircut. Guys, try to avoid facial hair—especially in conservative environments. Gals, wear a little make-up. No bar scenes with you holding a drink, looking goofy, or making out with your boyfriend or girlfriend. This is serious business. Mike, a smart, talented client, actually had a job offer rescinded after his prospective employer saw some objectionable pics on Mike's Facebook page.

Personalized URL. An absolute must-have, so people can easily find you. For LinkedIn, try to set up your profile URL so it's linkedin.com/in/your name with no numbers or slashes after your name. Keep it simple. Depending on the type of work you're looking for, you might also want to set up your own website as a place to showcase your writing samples, research, photos, and so on.

A single phone number where you can always be reached. I recommend the cell phone that you carry 24/7. Record your outgoing message in your own voice and simply state that you're not able to talk right now. Ask callers to please leave their phone number and say that you'll call back as soon as you're able. Your voice should be strong, confident, calm, and upbeat. Speak slowly and clearly and say, "Hello," not "Hi." Don't sing or rap, and make sure you don't accidentally (or deliberately) record traffic noise, barking dogs, or your kids shouting in the background. Your outgoing message may be a prospective employer's first contact with you, and it needs to make a positive, lasting impression. Finally, set your voicemail to pick up after no more than three rings. More than that and people may just give up and move on to the next resume in their pile.

A few words about phone etiquette: If your phone rings and you're not able to have a decent conversation, try to answer it anyway and tell the caller that you'll ring back at a time that's good for them. That said, do not answer the phone if you're in the restroom. (I know, you can't believe I'm actually mentioning this, but you'd be amazed at the stories I've heard…) If possible, explain why you can't talk— you're sitting in a dentist's chair, coaching your daughter's volleyball team, etc. That's less likely to make people feel that you're blowing them off to do something that's more important than speaking with them.

Advisory board. Staying around positive people is a must. And being with positive people who know you and support you is even better. Think about asking three or four people you trust to be your informal advisory board. The idea is to get their advice, bounce ideas off them, get their input on your action plan, and be around "positive speak." Meet with them periodically, face to face, and don't be shy about asking for help. It's hard to be "up" all the time, and sometimes you just need to be recharged. Don't forget to bring a dead mouse! Could be flowers, chocolates, pretty stamps, note cards, or just some info. But don't go empty-handed. Remember: optimism is one of the keys to success.

Okay, I know you're anxious to get out there and start setting up meetings. And you're almost there. But before you can pick up the phone, there's one more thing we need to do: make sure that the product you're trying to sell—you—looks, sounds, and acts as well as it possibly can. Ready for the next step?

Key Takeaways

♦ Know the tools of the trade. Besides your resume, you'll need a good email address, a customizable cover letter, and business cards.

♦ Come up with three good bullet points instead of a resume when trying to set up networking meetings.

♦ Set up—and complete—a good, professional-looking LinkedIn profile.

♦ Organize an advisory board of trusted people who will give you advice and positive reinforcement.

Chapter 4

Managing Your Presence

First impressions are lasting impressions—and you get only one chance to make one. That's why you should always—and I do mean always—be first-impression-ready. Think of it as the Power of Ten: The critical components of your first impression are the first 10 seconds people lay eyes on you, the first 10 steps you take toward them, and the first 10 words out of your mouth.

Despite all the stuff people say about not judging a book by its cover, the fact is that people (and by "people," I mean "anyone who's in a position to hire you") do exactly that every day.

My client Scott was having coffee with a person he had been introduced to via email, by a former colleague. Coincidentally, Scott was meeting with me first. When I saw him in his slacks and shirt, I asked if he had hung up the suit jacket in the office closet. When he looked perplexed, I explained that a suit and tie was appropriate attire for all meetings. You don't know who these people are, who they know, or whether they themselves are a hiring manager. Make a great first impression at all times, and know that it begins with what you're wearing to that first meeting. When in doubt, overdress. Better that than underdressed. You don't get a chance to do these meetings over. Once it doesn't go well, you're through. Anything we can do to build relationships and have meetings go well is something we should be doing.

Another client, Edgar, dressed impeccably every day, no matter where he went. And one day, that really paid off. When a recruiter contacted us and asked for a CPA, I immediately started calling clients. Edgar wasn't at the very top of my list, but the first two said they needed to go home to get changed before they could make the meeting, and the third candidate didn't answer her cell phone. But the recruiter needed the CPA yesterday. Edgar was ready to roll. He looked the part, got the meeting—and the job. Similarly, my client Brian had 185 "coffees" and was in a suit for all of them. He eventually landed a great job. Ken, on the other hand, liked to wear jeans and a

T-shirt. Unfortunately, he was looking for a corporate job, and very few of the people who saw him or networked with him referred him to others—a truly fatal problem.

I'm sure you've heard the expression, "Dress for success." But what, exactly, does that mean? Well, to start with, "dressing" involves a lot more than just clothes. The "cover" people are so carefully judging includes your posture, how you walk, how you talk (vocabulary, loudness, softness, level of confidence, intonation, speed), and, of course, your personal hygiene.

When You're On, You're On, and When You're Off, You're On, Too

As I always tell my clients, you're always on—even when you think you're off. What I mean is that people are watching you all the time—as they approach you when you're in the waiting room, when you're talking to the receptionist, when you're washing your hands in the restroom, and any other time you can think of. Imagine that all eyes are on you from the minute you step outside your home, and that everything you do until you get back and pour yourself into bed is being recorded (given the state of technology these days, that's probably true). You want that imaginary person who's reviewing the videos of your life to say, "Wow—she's fantastic!"

Ultimately, the success or failure of your dress will depend on the industry sector and the culture of the organization you're trying to fit in with. What works in New York probably won't work in Japan, and might not even fly in Chicago. If you've got an interview with a start-up, walking in with a scruffy half-beard, a nose ring, or tattoos that peek out over your collar might be perfectly fine. But if your interview (even if it's only an informational one) is with someone at a Big 4 accounting firm or with a congressman from Nebraska, the same look would probably get you stopped by security before you even get to the elevator. The same goes for the clothes you wear. Bottom line: When going into an office, make sure you're dressed the way people who work there dress.

When interviewing, networking, or having an informational meeting, please remember to keep buttoned up and professional at all times. Don't get comfortable, slouch, or use slang (unless it's industry specific). This is work, not play, and, except in very rare circumstances, people you're meeting with are not your friends—and don't let yourself get lulled into thinking they are. So full battle dress, guard up. Even if it's just an informational interview or networking meeting, every meeting is important and you should consider each as a potential interview. You never know whom they know or might be able to introduce you to. Ask good questions, have attentive body language, and smile. Be cognizant and respectful of their time and make the few minutes they share with you interesting and enjoyable. People hire people they like. Would the person you're talking with want to sit next to you on the red-eye back from the West Coast? If not, you may not be making your best impression. Always be professional, poised, and deferential. Always. That said, here are a few general ground rules that I advise you to keep in mind at all times.

Look young. Unfortunately, despite the fact that it's illegal for employers to discriminate on the basis of age, it's harder to find a job if you're over 40—even more so if you're over 50.

Act young, too, but don't go overboard. Have presence and energy but don't over-use slang or get too casual at a meeting.

Be nice—to everyone. That means the security guards in the parking lot, the receptionist, the administrative assistant, even the waitress at the coffee shop where you meet. You may not be interviewing with them, but believe me, if you treat them badly, the person you are interviewing with will hear about it. You just don't know who they are, whom they're related to, and whose ear they've got. And remember, there are cameras everywhere.

A classic, well-fitting suit made from a nice fabric is always in style. Crisp is good, and if your slacks or shirt are supposed to have creases, make sure they do. Go with a white or blue shirt and a non-neon silk tie in the red or blue family. Red is a conservative color and blue shirts tend to make men look younger. Try to mimic the dress code of the firm you are going to. Look at their websites, annual reports, and podcasts to see what the leaders and staff wear.

For men, hair should be relatively short. For women, contemporary and chic—and watch the color and roots.

For men, a clean-shaven look is best, unless you're up for a "hip" or "creative" job where stubble is common. Otherwise, facial hair tends to make men look older, so avoid it in any conservative environment (unless you look like you're 17 and need to put on a few years).

For women, less is usually more. Wear simple makeup—lipstick, mascara, and blush—and simple accessories, like one ring, post earrings and a simple chain, scarf, or pin. Keep it professional—statement jewelry can be lovely, but may send the wrong message in a conservative environment, so limit yourself to one piece. Carry only one bag and make sure you pack it with nothing more than essentials. Bulges are definitely out. Remember, some color is important, so don't go all black. Memorable is hireable.

Always wear a watch. No, not a Mickey Mouse, and leave the fake (or the real) Rolex at home.

Shine your shoes and make sure they don't look run-down. Gentlemen, be sure to check the heels of your shoes and your socks.

Brush your teeth and carry mints. I shouldn't have to tell you that, but you'd be amazed at how many people don't get it. You may find yourself in pretty close quarters with others, and the last thing you want them to be thinking about is how to end the interview and get a breath of fresh air. Oh, and floss is your friend. Enough said.

Take a picture of yourself dressed for a job interview or important networking meeting. Ask three trusted people (hello, advisory board!) to give you some honest feedback. And take a good, long look at yourself in a full-length mirror. Turn all the way round. Look sideways and in the back. Do you look professional, polished, and poised? I still picture myself as 29 and a size 8.

When meeting with people, be enthusiastic but not frenetic, engaged without seeming desperate. And above all, come across as knowledgeable about technology and social media. If you aren't already, spend some time getting yourself up to speed. Joking about how you're a technophobe or reminiscing about mimeographing or faxing on thermal paper isn't funny. And it pegs you as hopelessly out of date.

Show that you're flexible and open to new things. If you're taking a challenging class or just got back from a hiking trip, talk about it (but you might want to skip over the month-long African safari or the trek up Everest—you risk coming across as wealthy or entitled, qualities that employers generally aren't looking for). Don't talk about every book you read—we all read so there's nothing terribly special about that—unless you can discuss a great, non-business book you think your audience would be interested in.

Conquering Your Obstacles So You Can Get Hired

Everyone has an obstacle (or two, or three, or more) that may keep them from getting hired. Knowing what yours are and solving them is very important in this process—and very hard to do. For example, is it your age (or the age you look)? The fact that you are not an agile learner? In a world where we are all being asked to do more with less, you've got to be flexible and wear a lot of hats. Have no real subject-matter expertise? One of the key elements

Job Seekers over 50

I'm not sure how it happened, but old age is apparently starting a lot younger these days. Not all that long ago, you couldn't join the American Association of Retired People (AARP) unless you were 65. Over time, the cutoff gradually slipped to 55, then 50, and now it's 40! Wow, who knew! What this means is that when you're out there looking for a job, it's critical to come across as both young at heart as well as physically young. To help you fight ageism, I'll give you the same advice I give to my over-50 clients: Take a long, careful look at your:

- ♦ **Hair—and not just what's on your head** (which you should check for color, length, and style. If you're not sure, ask a 20-something to give you some feedback). Check your nose and ears for hair too.
- ♦ **Skin.** The smoother the better. If you aren't using moisturizer, you really should start—probably something with a little SPF. And be especially cognizant of your hands, since you'll be shaking hands with a lot of other people. And guys, pull your socks up. Nobody wants to see a bunch of skin when you cross your legs.
- ♦ **Weight.** Sadly, getting a job is about more than your qualifications. If you're overweight, I'm sure you're quite familiar with weight-shaming or discrimination in hiring. If you're over 50 and overweight, it's going to be a lot worse. I'm a big Weight Watchers fan, but do whatever it takes to get to your appropriate, healthy weight.
- ♦ **Posture.** Stand up straight, just like Mom told you.
- ♦ **Attire.** Go through your closet, and if you see any clothes from the '80s—like those blue shirts with the white collars, or pants with pleats or cuffs—donate them to Goodwill or put them into storage until they come back in style, which will eventually happen. But for now, they're gone, gone, gone.

- **Briefcase and accessories.** No one carries golf umbrellas anymore or wears a trench coat with the wool collar still attached.
- **Talk technology.** Be sure you have a smartphone (a tablet's a good idea too), and keep your calendar online. And don't be afraid to mention your Facebook page or LinkedIn profile (again, just be sure it's at least 90 percent complete). If you blog or tweet, say so (assuming it's safe for public consumption). Know what Tumblr is. My client Will's passion for baseball helped him land a job after a prospective manager stumbled onto his blog.
- **Language.** I occasionally have clients who spend a lot of time talking about Kidder Peabody, Salomon Brothers, and other companies that disappeared more than 20 years ago. Talking about the good old days reminds people of your age. It may also give them some (hopefully false) insight into where your head is at, along with the (also hopefully false) impression that you're still living in the past.

in your job search is learning how to build rapport with all types of people. My client Maura told me how she thought that looking for a job was a lot like speed dating. I agree! You meet a ton of folks, most of whom you're not going to marry (or even have a second date with), but you must meet them, make a good impression, learn about them. Whether they're your next hiring manager or not, you'll at least have them in your Rolodex and as LinkedIn contacts. A job search is about being uncomfortable. What could be less comfortable than a first date when you have no idea whom you're meeting? As I've said, it's a numbers game. But it's also a quality game, meaning that it's better to have 10 meetings than five, but better still to have five good ones than 10 bad ones. You control this!

Smile, use their name, have mutual interest points, and be authentic and warm. They have to like you! Remember to ask a question or two about them. Thanks to the Internet, there's no excuse for not doing your homework and stalking them (a tad).

One particularly common obstacle I see among clients is an obsession with job titles. Mark, for example, was a managing director at his former company and turned down several positions because the titles were (in his mind) lower status. But do you want a job or a title? Over the past few years, there's been a trend towards "juniorizing," meaning that what used to be a managing director role is now called a director, and executive VPs of old are now called senior VPs. The responsibilities are still the same; only the titles are different. No one's quite sure why this is happening—but does it really matter? Again, do you want a job or a title?

As I've said, there are very few do-overs in the job-search world. People are too busy for you to call them back and say, "Okay, I did that really poorly…" or, "Can I send you a new resume?" or, "Would you mind introducing me to your boss again?" I think not. So be sure to do your homework about the individual and the company you're meeting with—both online and in person if possible. And take as much time as you need to get your look, your pitch, your voice, and everything else in top shape before you walk into that meeting. You'll be glad you did.

Here's a list of other obstacles I see fairly frequently. In some cases, clients are aware of their obstacles. In other cases, they have no idea. As you read through this list (which is by no means exhaustive), do a little honest soul-searching. It's best to identify—and learn to overcome—any obstacles you may have before you start setting up meetings and interviews.

- Not knowing you have one
- Your age
- Negative speak
- Bad body language
- Lack of skills
- Lack of technology
- Poor references
- Overpaid
- Underpaid
- Same firm for years and years
- Overtalker
- Extremely nervous
- Bad reputation
- Not mindful
- Poor follow-up
- Short stints
- Shy/introvert
- Low energy
- Bankruptcy or bad background check possible
- Arrogant/know-it-all personality
- Poor communication skills
- Poor test-taking skills
- Poor interview skills
- Inability to build rapport
- Poor closings
- No strategic follow-up
- Same firm for 15 years

Key Takeaways

- Remember the Power of Ten: The critical components of your first impression are the first 10 seconds people lay eyes on you, the first 10 steps you take toward them, and the first 10 words out of your mouth.

- Dressing for success involves a lot more than your clothes. It includes your behavior, the language you use, your weight, your hygiene, and everything else.

- You get only one chance to get it right—there are very few do-overs in the job-search world.

Chapter 5

Your Job-Search Action Plan

Tom had the best job-search action plan I had ever seen. On the first page, he identified his job functions, where he had worked, what his accomplishments were, and included clear examples of his differentiation. On the second page, he included information on some community service projects he was involved in, and his interest in sports—great conversation starters—along with a list of the sectors and firms within those sectors where he would like to work. With his action plan and verbal positioning all set, Tom was able to use them as a roadmap for his successful job search. Ryan's was also fantastic, with visuals that made it simple and attractive. He also included metrics and plenty of active verbs and differentiators.

One of the most important components of your job-search action plan is a comprehensive list, similar to the ones Tom and Ryan put together, of companies you'd like to reach. As we discussed earlier, it's important to understand your strengths, your skill sets, what you can do to help your potential employer, your value proposition or USP (unique selling proposition), and your personal brand. Using that as a base, you'll start thinking about companies where the unique package you have to offer (you, of course) would best fit. Having this in mind will give you a jumping-off point.

Start by putting together the names of companies that are similar to the one you just came out of. Write down some of the ancillary firms that provide services to that sector, smaller companies in the same category, privately held ones, or private equity firms that have your type of company in their portfolio. Perhaps your previous clients and customers might be potential targets for you.

Keep in mind, though, that your list isn't (and should never be) set in concrete. Some of the options you're interested in will disappear, while new ones will open up. Don't let this throw you. As long as your list has more than 10 companies on it at a time, you're okay. Your ability to roll with the tide while keeping a positive outlook and optimistic attitude will separate you from the mob of disgruntled, dissatisfied, disenfranchised job hunters who are competing with you for the same jobs.

And don't rule out the possibility of a complete career shift. One client, Bernie, left an operations job to open a franchise; Richard went from a financial services firm to a hospital; Beth left a sales job to go to nursing school; Callie went from a bank to a cultural organization; Desireé made the leap from financial services to a small tech firm; and Sue was able to land a job with a private equity firm, despite never having worked for one before. As long as you know what you're good at and what motivates you (which is all part of the inventory we talked about in Chapter 1), you may discover other areas where your skills are applicable. All you need to learn is what's possible. Then add that information to your action plan options. If you haven't already done so, read *What Color is Your Parachute?* It's a great job-hunting resource.

The exercise of writing out your action plan will help you stay focused by keeping your list of target companies and individuals in front of you at all times. That's important because, given that it often takes forever to set up meetings, following your plan will allow you to pursue multiple goals at the same time, and will help identify your most logical next steps. A simple spreadsheet also helps you track your job search. You don't want to drop any balls or forget to follow through on a lead someone gives you. If you get a referral, be sure to contact that person within 48 hours of getting their information, and drop a note to the person who gave you the lead to let them know how it all turned out. They'll appreciate you circling back to them, and that, in turn, will make them more likely to give you other referrals. Again, it's all about how you make others feel.

Using Your Job-Search Action Plan

As we discussed in Chapter 3, you should not pull out your resume in an informational or networking meeting. You don't want your target to switch to "I've-got-to-get-this-guy/gal-out-of-my-office" mode. But do talk about your action plan. The person you're meeting with might have contacts at one or more of the firms on your target list, or, better yet, contacts at a company you never even thought of. If you're using your action plan as a conversation starter, your target may also be able to give you some valuable advice about better ways to highlight your skills, and even how to add in skills you hadn't thought to include in the plan. That's exactly what happened to Michael, who used his action plan in more than 70 meetings before successfully landing a great job.

If you can smoothly fit it into the conversation, ask if there's anyone else at the firm that they would feel comfortable introducing you to—for informational purposes only. You're trying to build a campaign within the firm even though there is officially no role. Companies create new roles all the time when they come across the right candidate: you! However, try not to talk too much about other firms or ask for referrals to other people until you're completely sure that the company you're meeting with isn't interested in you.

One last thought: at networking meetings, informational interviews, and formal interviews, people ask questions that they hope will get you to tell the truth about yourself. They're trying to see if you are negative and bitter, or honest, a team player, and a good fit with their organization. Be careful! For example, "You sound like you did a great job with that project. Why didn't they keep you on after the merger?" This speaks to your ability to not get defensive or speak negatively about your former employer or bosses. Detox before you embark on looking for that new or better job. People can see through bad karma, even when you think you're hiding it well. Or, "What is your number one weakness?" This is looking for someone who is a grown-up and self-aware and knows he or she is not perfect and is willing to admit it. This is where you might say, "I'm very focused on the details and sometimes I need to step back to see the forest instead of just the trees," or, "I'm sometimes impatient, but I know it all needs to be a collaborative effort and I'm working hard on breathing in and out and not snapping or sighing at anyone." This tells them you can be picky, but also that you're trying to mitigate it and overcome your weakness. Or they might ask, "What would your subordinates (or your peers or your boss) say about you?" This is about your operating style. Are you a role model, a mentor, a collaborative worker? A good answer is, "They'd say I'm a great leader who works hard to give credit to everyone else on the team and focuses on results and professional development."

Try out your action plan first on your network that knows you and get some valuable feedback and suggestions. I remember bringing mine to a networking lunch with my old boss, and he said, "You're missing one of the best things about you: your uncanny ability to bring out the best in others." I quickly added that attribute to my action plan.

Key Takeaways

♦ When putting together your job-search action plan, start with companies that are similar to the one you just left.

♦ Think about answers to questions you're likely to get in interviews or networking meetings.

♦ Be sure to detox before you embark on looking for that new or better job. People can see through bad karma, even when you think you're hiding it well.

Chapter 6

Charlotte's Web: Network or Not Work

At last! Francine was finally meeting the hiring manager she'd been trying to see for months. On previous calls, he'd mentioned his love for poker, and had even invited her to join his game (she declined, as she plays poorly!). Before their face-to-face meeting, she purchased a small set of poker chips and presented them to the manager. Memorable? You bet. And remember, memorable is hireable.

Somewhere along the way, networking got a dirty name. Let's understand that networking is merely speaking with another person and building rapport. In this chapter, the goal is to help you construct the road that will ultimately lead to getting hired. Don't worry; we'll start traveling down that road soon. Right now, though, we're focusing on networking, which is about building reciprocal, long-lasting relationships, not asking people for a job. More than 75 percent of my clients landed jobs through networking—not sitting online, not posting their resume, not relying on others or search firms, and certainly not applying for roles online.

Since the majority of all jobs aren't posted, odds are that you'll find your next position (and probably the one after that) through your network—not through job postings or ads. Many of the jobs posted have actually already been filled, but no one has taken the time to remove the posting. Or they have an internal candidate already slated for that role—and there's no beating an internal candidate. With companies unable to provide the high salaries or perks they could in the past, they're doing all they can to keep their top talent. So if a high performer inside the organization sees an opening they want, they can normally obtain it over an outsider. There's this wonderful "hidden" job market where there's work to be done but no headcount approved.

Remember: "no" really means "not now," so stay in touch! Companies are always looking for good talent. And when they find it, they somehow miraculously find the money to hire that terrific candidate. Paul was up for a great position and met with eight different people in the company. Unfortunately, he didn't get the job. But he stayed in touch with two of the managers he'd met with, and a few months later, he got a call from one of them about a job that was a much better fit!

Actually, in most cases, the people in your direct network won't have a job for you. What they do have, though, is even more important: networks of their own. The math is pretty simple: Having 10 people in your network is great. But if each of those 10 has his or her own network of 10, you're already up to 100 possible connections. And if each of those 100 has a 10-person network, you're up to 1,000 in no time. In my experience, the connection that leads to the job is usually between three and six degrees of separation from you. Don't have a network yet? Well, you'd better get cracking. Sara had 167 face-to-face meetings with her network and her network's network before she landed her perfect job.

When you're looking for a job, there's no need to suffer in silence. The more people who know, the better your chances of finding what you're looking for. People want to help, so let them! Start with your family, in-laws, friends, neighbors, people from your place of worship, parents of your kids' friends (you'll make a lot more connections on the sidelines of a soccer field than on a golf course). Reach out to colleagues and bosses from all of your previous jobs, not just the most recent ones—people who "grew up" with you professionally—and don't forget about vendors, suppliers, and clients you may have worked with in the past. Ask these people whom they know, and for referrals to others they respect, admire, or think might be open to a conversation with you.

And don't prejudge your network. Contact everyone—everyone knows someone, and it never hurts to ask. We all need to practice our pitch and meet new people. Ask for the contact or referral and then say yes to meetings. You just never know. If someone says, "I can introduce you to… Would that be helpful?" say yes. That person undoubtedly has a network, so you can then go further afield from your initial network circle.

There are lots of other ways to build your network. For example, check out alumni organizations (high school, college, and grad school), join an adult sports league, start going to meetings and conferences put on by professional associations and trade groups. See if you can sign on to be a speaker or panelist, introduce the speakers or panelists, or ask the organizers about volunteering. There are also dozens of groups that cross business sector lines. Some are organized by functionality (Risk Management Association, Financial Managers Association, International Association of Business Communicators, Financial Executives International, Marketing Executives Networking Group, Technology Executives Networking Group, Financial Executives Networking Group); gender (Financial Women's Association, 85 Broads, 100 Women in Hedge Funds, New York Women in Media and Television, etc.); ethnicity (100 Black Men, Asian American Federation, the Diversity Consortium, etc.); volunteerism (Kiwanis, Rotary, etc.); educational institutions (alumni associations, Phi Beta Kappa chapters, etc.); or even geographical location. Volunteer at a not-for-profit and meet other volunteers, staff, and the board. Add them to your networking list.

By now you should have quite a healthy list of people whom you know from a myriad of sources. The list will grow and change. Ask for referrals and add those (don't forget to send them LinkedIn invites when appropriate) to your networking list. I don't connect to strangers or people I've never met or spoken with, but I had one client who connected with over 800 strangers. To each his own, but I like to know my network and feel comfortable that when someone says, "Would you please introduce me to Diana?" I know whom they are talking about. Either way, keep track and have some kind of metric. "Have I added three new people to my LinkedIn this week?"

Networking, Step by Step

"Networking" is one of those words that we've all heard—and think we understand. But in my experience, it's more than just a word, or even a concept. Instead, it's a methodical, five-step process.

1. Identify the target
2. Contact the target
3. Do your research
4. Have the meeting
5. Follow up tenaciously

Let's take a look at each of these steps in detail.

1. Identify the Target

Now that you have a pretty good handle on your network, put together a list of every company that you might like to work for. Does anyone you know or worked with in the past work there now? Used to work there? Does anyone in your network know someone who works or used to work there? As I mentioned above, the majority of jobs aren't posted, so networking is the best way of finding out what's out there. There's a whole hidden job market. So send emails out and ask.

Some people are natural networkers—they always seem to be making personal and professional connections. At one point, my client Carolyn had 64 networking meetings in one week, and Justin had nearly 200 over just a few months! Granted, most of these took place at networking events where there were a lot of people to meet with, but Carolyn and Justin thrive in reaching out to strangers.

Unfortunately, most of us are far from natural networkers. Fortunately, as with so much else in life, it's more about quality than quantity. Sure, having five to seven face-to-face meetings every week is great—if you can do it. But even if you have only two or three, try to make each one as productive and fruitful as possible. Never go without thinking through the agenda. When you were working, did you ever put together a meeting without an agenda? I think not!

2. Contact the Target

When trying to set up a meeting, don't try to reach the referral directly unless you absolutely have to. Having your contact (or your contact's contact) make the introduction is a much more powerful way to go in than your making a cold call and saying, "Hi, I was referred by Sue Smith. Do you have time next Tuesday?" However, as soon as the initial introduction has been made, reach out yourself right away. In most cases, you'll start with a quick email and then follow up with a phone call. But find out your target's preferred mode of communication and do it that way—not what's easiest for you.

Email is always easy, but it's not ideal. It's passive and we all get hundreds of them every day. If there's no alternative, at least be sure to put something meaningful into the subject line—such as the name of the person who made the referral. Hopefully, that will keep your emails out of your target's SPAM box. Do not send your resume. Send your bullets. Nothing is more of a door-closer than sending your resume. People sometimes feel that you are asking them for a job, not a networking meeting. Be clear that you're not asking for a job.

Be pleasantly persistent and tenacious, but don't stalk. If you've tried three times (twice by email and once by phone) but haven't had any luck getting on your target's calendar, circle back with your initial contact. Understand that delays happen. It's easy to take someone's lack of responsiveness as a personal rejection, but it usually isn't. They're just busy doing their job. Or perhaps there's something going on that you don't know about. Give everyone the benefit of the doubt. After three weeks of getting absolutely nowhere with what had sounded like a really promising contact, my client Grant was getting frustrated and a little depressed. But after getting back in touch with the contact who had made the introduction, he found out that the woman he was trying to meet had been out of the office nursing her ailing husband.

Chances are you're reaching out to people with busy jobs who are being asked to pack even more work (including meeting with you) into what was already a pretty crazy schedule. Remember when you were working? How many times did you let that outreach or networking call or email slip to the next day, the day after that, or drop it altogether? You didn't do it out of spite; you were just plain busy.

Do not show your annoyance in emails or phone calls; try to relax and remember that job hunting is a numbers game. Keep sending emails and making those calls, and you'll probably get six out of 10 meetings. Some of them might be only a five-minute phone call, but if that's all you get, take it! Any incremental progress counts. And remember to invite these folks (when you think they'll be comfortable) via LinkedIn. One way to figure out whether to invite someone into your LinkedIn network is to ask yourself if you would be comfortable introducing them to your network. If not, take a pass.

Cutting the Cord

If the person you're reaching out to has never been unemployed or doesn't know anyone who has been, he or she may be slow to help or respond. They just don't "get it." After trying seven times (four emails and three phone calls) to get someone to speak with you or meet with you, and it doesn't happen, it's time to cut the cord. But do it actively, by sending a final email that says: "So sorry we were never able to connect or speak. All good wishes for a terrific year. Best regards, Steve."

There are three reasons to do this. First, you've been thinking that you have something going but you actually don't. So you might as well free up the space in your heart and brain and start focusing on a meeting that might actually happen.

Second, it empowers you. Sometimes in a job search, you feel a tad like a victim, quite vulnerable and with no control over anything. Taking the initiative and ending things puts you in the driver's seat. Third, it sometimes gets people to respond. Guilt can be a wonderful motivator! Just remember to always be polite, persistent, and nice. What goes around comes around... Always try to pay it forward. The reality is, if you live long enough, you'll see all kinds of neat stuff. Focus on being the very best you can be. Don't just do your best—do what's necessary to get it done. Always remember to ask yourself the most important job-search question: "How did I make them feel?"

3. Do Your Research

Okay, you've got the meeting. Fantastic. But now what? Well, first, congratulate yourself on completing the hardest part of the process! Next, start researching and doing due diligence about the person you're meeting with, the firm, and their business sector. Google is a good place to start, but don't end there. You can find a lot of great financial information on sites like Yahoo! Finance, Schwab, Vanguard, Bloomberg, and Motley Fool. Spend some time on the company's website, and read everything you can. For public companies, read the CEO's letter to shareholders (you'll find it in the company's annual report). Generally, in these communiqués, the CEO shares strategic plans for the coming fiscal year and will talk about the company's culture—very important background knowledge for your face-to-face meetings. Pull up the company's three most recent press releases so you're up to date on the latest developments.

Speak to people who have worked there, work there now, or who know the firm and its culture and products. The day of the interview, re-Google them and read up on any last-minute news stories. One client, Theresa, told me how she found out—while sitting on the train on the way to a meeting—that the company had just announced a major acquisition. Definitely good information to have. Steve told of an interviewer asking specifically about something that was on the front page of the newspaper that morning. Unfortunately, Steve hadn't read the paper that day! Remember to use social networking sites to learn more about your targets: associations they belong to, children they have, universities they attended, panels they've spoken on, articles they've written, and so on.

4. Have the Meeting

Once you get a meeting, it's critical to keep in mind that you're not there to talk about yourself or to ask for a job. In fact, the worst thing you can do is come right out and ask, "Do you have anything for me?" I know that this is a paradigm shift for most job seekers. After all, you do want a job, right? And it's tempting to talk about yourself, your accomplishments, and how perfect you'd be for the company. But don't. For now, all you're doing is building bridges, learning, and listening. Lots of active listening. As a rule, spend 80 percent of your time using your ears, 20 percent using your mouth. The more you know about the people you're meeting with and the circles they run in, the more likely you'll be able to make a specific request later. People hire people they like—and who like them.

By listening carefully, you're saying, "I get you; I like you; I'm interested in what you have to say and what you represent." My client Don met several people at the firm he was interested in and each of them passed him on to yet another person at the same firm. Soon, he had his "village" of inside champions and was offered a job! Campaign for what you want at firms that make sense for you. Don't worry whether there's a role open or not. If they like you enough, they'll open one for you.

There are three components to every networking meeting:

◊ The Give

◊ The Get

◊ The Get Out (next steps)

The Give is your gift to the person you're seeing—the famous dead mouse that's in the title of this book. No one gave more dead mice than my client Susan. Which is why she landed a terrific position in only 60 days—the only client I've ever had who found a job that quickly (remember, the average for senior execs is over 10 months). She helped more people in more ways than I could possibly count. If she saw a job online that she thought was a good fit for someone else, she sent it to that person; she sponsored people who wanted to be part of networking forums she was in or groups she belonged to; she connected people she thought would be useful and helpful to each other. Dead mice galore.

After the initial icebreakers, you present your dead mouse. My client Pooja once brought a small baby gift to a potential hiring manager she had met with several times. Remember, it's how you make them feel that counts. When you bring someone a gift that lets them know you're thinking of them, they, in turn, will think of you. It's human nature to reciprocate. You start, and whoever gets your gift will follow.

I spend about half my practice strategizing with clients about dead mice—how to identify them and present them without looking contrived. It doesn't have to be (and shouldn't be) anything big or expensive. It just needs to be thoughtful. Say, for example, you've got a meeting with a gal who's just about to send her oldest child off to college. If you've been in that spot yourself, a book, an article, or even some advice from a pro could be in order. My client Dan had read a great book about dads and daughters that he shared with many others during his job search. He even got the book signed by the author. Mike learned that his hiring manager was a history buff and sent her a great book. David sends the book he wrote on risk management. Of course, it doesn't have to be a book. Maybe you know the person you're meeting with is a Jets fan, and you bring an autographed cap.

Your dead mouse doesn't always have to be an actual object. One client, Joe, heard that a mutual colleague had recently changed jobs, and he passed that info along to the target, who was delighted to hear about his friend. That seemingly simple piece of information also gave the target the very clear message that Joe was a guy who's keeping up on the industry and its players. Another client, Rich, would identify other job seekers to a company if he wasn't the right fit. That established him as someone who was well-connected and cared enough about the company's success to refer good people to them.

The point here is that you're trying to differentiate yourself in a market where there are many, many more candidates than jobs. If you're not sure how to find appropriate dead mice, you can always set up Google Alerts to send you any information that shows up on the Web that mentions your target, companies you're looking into, business trends, and any other items of interest. Coming into a meeting with something (actual or metaphorical) can set the tone for the rest of the meeting and make the difference between an okay meeting and a truly stellar one. Put your target first, not yourself. What can you do to be helpful professionally or personally, so that you'll be seen as a resource? The key is to be absolutely authentic. If you're not, folks will know, and you'll be worse off than if you hadn't brought anything at all.

Scott met with a ton of people, asking for a role, job, or opportunity. But it wasn't until he started coming up with ideas of ways that he could help others that he began to get assignments—and then a job! Be creative and thoughtful—what can you do to be an extra pair of hands? What could they use you for now? Make a role for yourself. Never assume that other people will do it for you. Again, the key is to be absolutely authentic, but have a clear plan of action.

The Get is what you're asking for. Let's say the company you're meeting with is in the consumer package industry, and there are four companies you've identified that you'd like to speak with. Could your target introduce you to anyone at any (or all) of those companies? Not necessarily about a job—just to see what areas are growing and where the trends are.

Always pay attention to the person you're talking with and what he or she is doing. If the person is busy scribbling notes down on paper, they've disengaged from you. Stop talking, ask a question, and reel them back in. Watch your body language, smile, use their names, and go back to a part of the conversation where he or she was engaged. Rewind. Begin to figure out how to cut the meeting short and make a graceful and intelligent exit.

The Get Out comes toward the end of the meeting and is simply a way of keeping the conversation going. This could be giving the target a card, getting one of hers (try to get a business card from everyone you meet with, so you'll have their title, address, and correct spelling of their name— you'll need all that for your thank-you notes), or asking for a time when you should check back to see whether she was able to make the introductions you'd talked about. Also ask whether she prefers a phone call or email.

Have a very solid closing; it's how you'll be remembered. The key to all of this is to make your pitch during the meeting. Coming up with an idea and emailing it in two days afterwards won't do you much good. Too little, too late. Look for those opportunities and be ready to ask, "Would that be helpful? I'd love to do it and it should only take four days of work and six or seven meetings with your staff..." Give the idea or intellectual capital and get the work. Give to Get. However, be very careful. If you've put any of that intellectual capital down on paper, be sure to take it with you. Those fantastic ideas for how to improve the company's bottom line are yours and you should be the one to implement them.

Remember that many of the people you meet with are too overworked and overwhelmed to think about adding headcount or to come up with a project or an assignment for you. They barely have enough hours in the day to get their jobs done and get home at a decent hour to be with their family. In cases like this—when there doesn't seem to be a clear job for you—you need to think about how you're going to create value for them. For example, you meet a business manager who tells you she's having trouble getting all of her projects done on time and on budget. And as a seasoned project manager, you know all it takes is some workflow analysis and a methodology that fits with the company's work and platform. Offer to have a few conversations with her team and then put together an action plan they can implement. You'll include the timing, cost, and resources the manager will need to get the project done quickly and seamlessly, without disrupting the current work or making anyone uneasy with all of your questions (or your mere presence).

5. Follow Up Tenaciously

My mom always told me that I was brought up, not dug up—so act accordingly.

Within 24 hours after your meeting, be sure to send an email thank-you to the person you met with—if you met with 11, send out 11. If you're in doubt about whether to send a thank-you, send one. No one ever didn't land a job because she thanked too many people. On the other hand, there are plenty of people out there who didn't get jobs because they didn't send notes. Keep in mind that we're talking about thank-you notes, not notes about you, how wonderful you are, and how perfect you are for the job. Do not send joint or group emails; individualize and personalize them by mentioning something the other person spoke about. For example:

Dear Sonia,

Thanks so much for meeting with me today.

Your insights around Brexit and the impact on your business really resonated with me and are clearly ringing true.

Please let me know if I may provide anything additional. Have a great weekend.

Best regards,
Charlotte

Be sure to send handwritten thank-yous to the people who went to bat for you and set up meetings (because handwritten notes are uncommon, they really help you stand out—in a good way). You may need to keep in touch with them in case you need their help with future follow-through. In the meantime, get ready for your next meeting—and don't forget your dead mouse.

Key Takeaways

♦ Networking is merely speaking with another person and building rapport.

♦ Since the majority of all jobs aren't posted, odds are that you'll find your next position (and probably the one after that) through your network—not through job postings or ads.

♦ Don't prejudge your network. Contact everyone—everyone knows someone, and it never hurts to ask.

Notes

Chapter 7

Activity vs. Productivity

You used to wake up in the morning and go to work; now you just wake up. But remember the long hours you used to put into your job at the office? This is no time for slacking off. This isn't a vacation or a time to catch up on all of those chores you're behind on. If you really need to get things done around the house—and you can afford it—consider taking a month off to adjust to having lost your job and to take care of all those non-job-related things. Whether it's re-connecting with your family, going to visit your parents, taking French classes, or going on vacation, do it! Then you can jump in renewed and refreshed, and focus completely on your new, full-time occupation: finding work.

When you're in the midst of a full-blown job search, there are a million things to do. Make calls, send emails, go to networking conferences, check out job fairs, reach out to people who have been referred to you, work on and post your resume, get your LinkedIn profile perfect, and keep your tracking up to date. As we've discussed, it's taking most people longer to find a job these days than ever, so it's crucial that you use your time wisely. Right below this paragraph you'll find a chart with my suggestion for how to divide and categorize your efforts—in general terms. Take a look at it, and then I'll show you what a typical job-search schedule might look like.

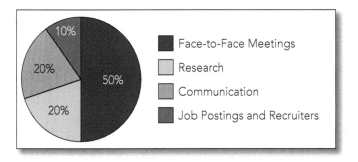

A few clarifications:

Face-to-face meetings. This includes networking, informational, or any other meeting that gets you out of your pajamas and out from behind your computer screen. As you spend more time on your job search, the face-to-face percentage should grow to about 75 percent of your time, with research, emails, and phone calls taking up the remaining 25 percent.

Research. Thinking through your target companies, knowing a lot about the firms and people you are going to see, understanding which industry sectors are growing or at least healthy.

Communications. Emailing, calling, inviting LinkedIn friends, thank-you notes, sending interesting articles.

Job postings, headhunters, and recruiters. Applying for positions, reaching out to five or six headhunters/recruiters. It's best if you can be introduced to these headhunters by someone who knows them, and that they, of course, cover your sector and function.

Structure your job-hunting workday in a very similar way to how you might have structured your on-the-job workday. My client Sandy was at his desk every morning at exactly 8:30, wearing a suit and tie. And I'm talking about when he was unemployed. Sandy took his job-hunting very seriously, spending his days meticulously hitting the phones, writing cover letters, sending emails, and setting up face-to-face meetings. On page 76 is an example of what a typical job-hunting daily schedule might look like.

It's very easy to fall into the trap of networking, making calls, and setting up meetings because you want to keep busy—and you want everyone to know that you're looking for a job. But there's a big difference between being truly productive and simply spinning your wheels. Here are some tips that will help you keep your job search focused, organized, and disciplined:

1. OHIO – Only Handle It Once (I stole this from my client Greg). Touch each piece of paper only once. Don't just move it around from place to place. Either deal with it immediately or file it away.

2. Make up your business cards once. Send the draft to two people you trust (career coach and friend who

works in the business sector you are pursuing) and get their comments. Then have the cards printed.

3. Send impactful, actionable emails so you'll get replies and answers the first time you reach out. Show one to someone on your advisory board and then you will have a template for your search going forward. For example:

Subject: Quick catch-up?

Good morning Brian,

Hope you are well and had a great New Year's holiday. I ran into Arun, who sends his regards. Sorry I've been out of touch; would you have time for a quick catch-up call or coffee?

Thanks, and best,
Charlotte
(555) 555-5555

---

4. Leave detailed voicemail messages—including a concise heads-up about why you're calling—so you can avoid endless rounds of telephone tag.

5. Track your job search to ensure your metrics are holding (are you making your target of 5–10 calls every day? Seven face-to-face meetings every week?). But don't spend too much time focusing on systems and complicated processes that take a lot of time and energy to complete. A simple

Excel spreadsheet or alphabetical listing by target, company, and/or name of contact is just fine. The easier it is to update, the more likely you'll actually use it. One of the most important reasons to have a good tracking system is so that, 30 people later, you still know how you got that contact and that job—and can thank everyone along the way.

6. Be careful that you're not scheduling meetings just for the sake of having meetings, and make sure you're not overbooking yourself. Adele had back-to-back meetings every day for months and was exhausted. When she switched some to phone calls—and eliminated others altogether—her search progressed a lot faster. Go through your calendar and make sure you're limiting yourself to no more than three in-person meetings per day. Also be sure that each of those in-person meetings has a purpose and agenda. If it doesn't, make it a phone call instead. If it still looks like it might fall flat, pull it off the calendar by telling the person you're meeting with that you're finishing up your job-search marketing plan and would like to circle back when it's done. Everyone's overbooked these days, and if the people you were scheduled to meet with can take one meeting off their calendar without feeling guilty about blowing you off, they'll be thrilled.

7. One of the best ways to ensure that you're always moving forward is to write your target companies down and give yourself a deadline of 60 days to have had conversations with all of them.

My Schedule for Today

7:00 am – 8:00 am	Wake up and work out (walk, run, swim, weights, yoga, meditate)
8:00 am – 8:30 am	Shower, breakfast, get dressed
8:30 am–10:30 am	Turn on phone, return calls, check emails and return those (be sure to carefully review your emails before clicking Send)
10:30 am – 11:30 am	Stand up, have tea, stretch, call a friend or someone from your Advisory Board*
11:00 am – 11:30 am	Change into "work clothes" and head off to your lunch/ networking meeting
11:30 am -1:30 pm	Travel to your meeting, have your meeting, come home
1:30 pm–5:30 pm	Send a thank you note to your lunch partner, apply for one job online, send seven LinkedIn invites, answer emails, call four people to set up meetings for next week, research for your next meeting (interview, informational, etc.)**

*More about your Advisory Board in Chapter 3.
** Never schedule two meetings back-to-back. The first one may start late or run long, or you might get asked to meet more people or join them for lunch or a drink.

Triangulate if at all possible: have a stronghold in the target company who's your initial contact, but add two others in the organization who can advocate for you. The ideal is three advocates inside and three from the outside calling your "insiders" over a period of time... not all in one week. If at all possible, one of those insiders would be in HR, while the other two would be in the actual business lines (meaning non-HR positions).

8. Meet with someone on your advisory board twice a month to keep your feet to the fire and ensure you're keeping to your schedule. Then update your list to cross off contacts you've connected with and add new targets. Seek and embrace feedback. Ask how you're being perceived. Ask for advice on how to be more helpful, value-added, and current in this ever-changing market environment.

9. Be sure to build some "me time" into your day. You need to arrive at every meeting looking and feeling your very best. So whether it's the gym in the morning, a midday walk, or an evening swim, do whatever keeps you of sound mind and body. Our stress shows on our face and on our body.

Key Takeaways

- When you're in the midst of a full-blown job search, there are a million things to do. It's taking most people longer to find a job these days than ever, so it's crucial that you use your time wisely.

- Be careful that you're not scheduling meetings just for the sake of having meetings. Go through your calendar and make sure that each meeting has a purpose and agenda. Two to three good meetings per day is plenty.

- Be sure to build some "me time" into your day. So whether it's the gym in the morning, a midday walk, or an evening swim, do whatever keeps you of sound mind and body. Our stress shows on our face and on our body.

Chapter 8

Don't Fall in Love

During the job-hunting process, you're going to meet a lot of people and have interviews at a number of organizations. I know it's hard, but it's important to try not to fall in love with any of them (I'm talking about the companies, not the people—although falling in love with the people probably isn't a very good idea either). Austin spent three months focused on one specific financial services firm. But one day he found out that the person whose job he was hoping to take over had decided not to leave the company after all. Poof! In a nanosecond, Austin's perfect job disappeared. Mike spent two and a half months pursuing one job with a large firm and they ended up hiring the other guy.

Rich was convinced that Big Bank was going to hire him. They asked all the right questions (when can you start?) and said all the right things (we really need you here—you'll fit in perfectly…) but they didn't. Fortunately, Rich kept a few other balls in the air and kept going to networking meetings, and a smaller, but more profitable investment bank hired him a few weeks later. Mark, on the other hand, was the job-hunting equivalent of a serial monogamist who fell in love four times in a row. He actually knew by the third time that he was doing it, but he couldn't help himself. He over-prepared, over-thought, dropped other leads and networking meetings, and ended up prolonging his search by months.

The moral of the story is: Until you've got a signed employment letter in hand, or you've got your new office key and are ordering business cards and hiring an assistant, keep your options open. Once the job is in the bag, you can go back to your old habits (I hope you won't) but at least until then, keep meeting with lots of folks, practice and refine your pitch, improve your presentation, and adjust your style for many different audiences.

How many? In my experience, five is a good number. It's nice to have two positions that are pretty well developed, and three more in the pipeline. This way, as job opportunities come and go—and they always do—you've still got some hot and warm prospects. If you're trying to bubble them up at the same time, tell the others that you're "close" to a verbal offer and you were wondering what their timing might be. That will signal to them that you're interested and to get moving if they're interested in you. Try not to give them an ultimatum or say that you have an offer, as they may step back and say, "Okay, go for it. We'll take a pass."

This kind of approach comes naturally to sales people— they know that they need to be working 10 possibilities at the same time, because chances are only one will pan out. Same for you. Continue to network and keep those irons in the fire. It builds capacity around your search in general. Plan a trip out of town to meet with former colleagues, clients, or customers. If you're in New York, you can easily hit Philadelphia, Stamford, Washington, D.C., or Boston. If you're in Chicago, don't overlook Minneapolis. In LA? Go to San Francisco and San Jose, too. This gets your name out there more widely, helps you keep current, and helps you bring your personal brand to the market.

The more your name is out there, the better off you are. People talking about you and seeing you as a potential connector or a resource is great. For example, Dave was unemployed but when a publicly traded company was looking to hire someone, they called him. Turns out his name had been given to them twice, in two different situations. It's less about falling in love and more about speed dating—until you get the job. Then it's the real thing. (We'll talk more about the process of onboarding at your new job in Chapter 12.)

Not being in love also helps you negotiate. We'll talk a lot more about that in Chapter 10.

After you've landed that new job, be sure to go back and reconnect with the people you met with and who made connections for you. Now that you have a role, you have good news to share with them in person. People don't want to feel you just contacted them because you were out of work and needed something. Try to stay in touch with people when you already have a job and don't need anything. It merely takes a LinkedIn message, email, phone call, or holiday card. That's true friendship.

Finally, nothing lasts forever. Same goes for this job. Chances are, you won't retire from this job unless you're 67 or older and/or you don't need or want to work. So stay optimistic, but keep your options open and continue to build relationships. And never, ever get complacent or stop networking. Remember the old adage, "You're not in a job; you're just between job searches."

Key Takeaways

- Don't put all your eggs in one basket. Things don't always work out the way you hope they will.

- Until you've got a signed employment letter in hand, or you've got your new office key and are ordering business cards and hiring an assistant, keep your options open.

- After you've landed that new job, be sure to go back and reconnect with the people you met with and who made connections for you.

Chapter 9

Working with Recruiters and Headhunters

At a recent networking event, Ben told the other 30 out-of-work people in the room that if he had to do it over again, he would have spent less time with recruiters. A lot less. Why? Simply put, recruiters are not your friends. They may woo you and may take you out to lunch, and may sound encouraging and upbeat. But they work for the employer—not for you—and they don't always have your best interests at heart. I'm not saying they're deliberately trying to deceive you—it's just that their loyalties lie with the company that will be paying their fee (which they often earn only after they make the placement), not with you. And in order to earn that fee, the recruiter or headhunter will wine and dine as many possible candidates as it takes. For them it's a numbers game. If they contact enough people, eventually they'll find the right candidate.

Unless you're very senior, or you have a very narrow focus or functionality, you should be spending 90 percent of your job-hunting time developing leads from your own network, and only 10 percent working with headhunters and recruiters.

If you do get a call from a headhunter, the first thing you want to ask is whether he or she is working on a "retained search." That means that the recruiter has an exclusive arrangement with the hiring company (those recruiters/head-hunters are typically quite sophisticated and are the "real deal"). With retained searches, even if an internal candidate is selected, the headhunter is paid a fee. In non-retained searches, the hiring company client has put the word out to a number of recruiters, and whoever brings in the right candidate gets the fee. In situations like these, the recruiter who's calling you is conducting a bit of a fishing expedition. So ask who the client (hiring company) is, what the position is, what it pays, and whether the search is retained or contingency. If they can't (or won't) answer all of those questions, don't bother sending your resume. On the other hand, if you get a sense that the recruiter is truly plugged in and has some real market intel, try to schedule a face-to-face meeting.

Once you find out the name of the company, you might discover that you're already speaking with them, or that you had submitted your resume for a job online. Coming at a company from several different directions makes you look disorganized and desperate. No employer wants to pay recruiter fees. If you made it onto their radar on your own or through your network, they'll save a lot of money (up to one-third of the job's projected annual salary).

More often than not, the job a recruiter is calling about won't be right for you anyway. It might be for a position that's too junior, requires more travel than you're willing to accept, or skills you don't have. If that's the case, don't just hang up the phone; instead, try to take advantage of having the recruiter on the phone and turn the call to your advantage.

One excellent way to do that is to recommend someone who might be a better candidate than you. If you don't know anyone, search your network and try to find someone who would be appropriate for the role. Or email or call a friend or colleague who might have an idea. That way, you'll come across as responsive, well-connected, and willing to help the recruiter land that big fee. You can be sure that the next time a position that's got your name on it comes along, that recruiter will call you first. And who knows, the person you recommended for the job may return the favor by recommending you for something else or giving you a great contact.

Another reason to keep the recruiter on the phone is that recruiters are often great sources of market intelligence. Many of them come out of industry themselves, and they can give you the inside scoop on what's going on, whether it's something about the sector as a whole, or individual companies within that sector. The more you talk to recruiters (and the more you listen to their market insights), the more current you'll sound when you're in meetings or interviews. At the same time, take advantage of your contacts with worthwhile recruiters to boost your own stock. You're the subject-matter expert in your field, right? So share some market intel (as long as it's not proprietary, of course).

One last tip: Always be transparent in your search. If you're already talking to that firm, tell the recruiter. If they tell you about a job, don't go around them and approach the company directly. If you honestly hadn't met with that company before the headhunter mentioned it, let the headhunter take you in. Then you can call everyone you know there. Let the headhunter know about all of the people you know who work there now and any who used to work there. Going around a headhunter will backfire. You'll get a reputation in the market as someone without integrity—and that will tarnish your name, your reputation, and your brand. Do you really want to burn bridges in a tight job market or, frankly, in any job market?

Key Takeaways

- ♦ Recruiters are not your friends. They may woo you and may take you out to lunch, and may sound encouraging and upbeat. But they work for the employer—not for you.
- ♦ If a recruiter has a job that isn't right for you, consider recommending someone you know who'd be a good fit.
- ♦ Going around a headhunter will backfire. You'll get a reputation in the market as someone without integrity—and that will tarnish your name, your reputation, and your brand.

Chapter 10

Negotiation Dos and Don'ts

I've seen it over and over: Highly qualified, smart, talented people who land a dream job and then end up feeling resentful because they jumped at the offer without trying to negotiate a better deal. Believe me, I get it. You've been out of work for a while, you're tired of looking, you've got an offer to do exactly what you want to do (or at least pretty close to it), and you don't want to jinx the deal by asking for too much. That's perfectly understandable. It's also a big mistake.

The truth is that companies expect you to negotiate, and unless you ask for something completely insane (12 weeks of vacation, a maid and a chauffeur, a private zoo for your pet ocelot), it's extremely unlikely that attempting to negotiate all or part of an offer is going to jeopardize the prospective job. In fact, it's likely to have the opposite effect. Here's why:

◊ It shows initiative and leadership.

◊ It's often a sign of a candidate who will advocate for others since she advocates for herself.

◊ There's really no downside and nothing to lose.

However—and these are two big howevers—always:

◊ Be professional, gracious, and eloquent

◊ Negotiate in person or on the phone (never by email)

In much the same way as your job search started with trying to identify your priorities, so will your negotiations. Of course, I can't tell you what those will be, but here are some that many of my clients have put at the top of their list:

Have Data to Support Your "Asks"

You wouldn't (hopefully) walk into a job interview without at least having a pretty good handle on the company and its culture. You shouldn't walk into a negotiation without knowing whether what you're asking for is reasonable. The best way to find out is to spend some time gathering data. For example, most corporations have structured compensation programs with established salary ranges for most

Identifying Your Priorities

- Job title
- Starting date
- Cash compensation
- Sign-on and other bonus
- Commission
- Salary review in 30/60/90 days
- Stock
- Profit share, pension, 401k
- Medical, dental, vision
- Insurance (life, disability, accident)
- PTO/vacation/sick leave
- Paternity/maternity/ carryover
- Non-compete clause
- Expense account
- Relocation/travel
- Day care
- Housing assistance
- Professional/trade association membership or dues
- Conferences to attend
- Severance
- Club memberships
- Outplacement
- Automobile/commuting expenses
- University tuition grants
- Other company programs
- Flextime/alternate schedules

positions (although that may not be true for a start-up). You can usually find out a lot of what you need by researching publicly available sources. But the most important information will come from:

- ◊ Speaking to people who work inside the company
- ◊ Speaking to people who used to work in the company
- ◊ Speaking to professionals in the industry and comparable institutions

Pick Four and Ask

Once you've compared what the company's offering to what you might reasonably ask for, and you've identified and ranked your priorities, pick your top four and get ready. Start at the top of the range and be prepared to settle for less. For example, you might:

◊ Ask for $75k–$80k if you're prepared to take $65k

◊ Ask for five weeks of vacation if you're okay with four

◊ Ask to start in 30 days even though you could actually start next week

The most important thing here is to know what your "settle point" is. If the company can't or won't accept your counteroffer or meet you halfway, how much will you compromise? Is there a point at which you'll walk?

A Note about Money

Get paid at least what you made last year. Actually, start your negotiating by asking for 15% more than you made in your last job. Even if you don't get the full amount, there's a good chance that you'll get a bump. Getting a higher salary has to happen with a new job, not in a new job. It's the only time you have leverage. Be prepared to walk away (the job-hunting equivalent of the game of chicken) if they won't compensate you fairly. Do you really want to work at a place that undervalues its employees?

If Things Go as Well as You'd Hoped

Congrats! Follow up with a thank-you email confirming the changes you and the person you've been negotiating with have agreed upon. And, if you've been negotiating with HR, be sure to send an email to the hiring manager as well.

If Things Don't Go as Well as You'd Hoped (But You Still Want the Job)

Two important rules:

◊ Never sound disappointed. Be delighted and make sure everyone you're speaking with knows you're excited to be joining the team.

◊ Ask whether your salary (or whatever matters to you the most) can be revisited in three or six months.

If Things Don't Go as Well as You'd Hoped (And You're Prepared to Walk)

Never, ever, ever burn bridges. Follow up with a very polite email. You never know where people will end up, and you may find yourself in a few years sitting across a negotiating table with the same people. They wouldn't have offered you a job if they didn't think you were a top candidate. So make the best impression and, hopefully, they'll come to see that they missed a fantastic candidate.

Notes

Chapter 11

Special Situations

Over the many years I've been coaching executives, many of the big issues my clients face have stayed the same—they're the ones we've covered in the previous 10 chapters. But in recent years, I'm seeing a lot more people who fall into one of the four demographics that we'll talk about in this chapter:

◊ Young people who might still be in college but are thinking ahead to their first professional job

◊ People who've been out of work for a year or longer

◊ People who've been out of work for a lot longer—like a decade

◊ Veterans

Let's take a look at each of these groups.

Young People

At the risk of sounding like your mother, don't waste your college years.

That doesn't mean you can't enjoy yourself while you're in school. Of course you can—and should. But you should also think of those years as a great opportunity to get experience and skills that'll come in quite handy when you get that first (and second and third) big job. In particular, I'm talking about meeting new people, many of whom will help you expand and enhance your network.

Let's say, for example, that the fraternity or sorority that you're thinking about pledging has a regular community service project. Try to get on that project and work your way into a leadership role. If they don't have such a project, you should still consider volunteering or doing some kind of community service, particularly with not-for-profits with household names like Habitat for Humanity, the American Cancer Society, and Big Brothers Big Sisters.

And join clubs—as many as you can handle without sacrificing your grades. Doesn't matter whether it's economics, debate, politics, or something else; the point is to join and get to know as many people as you can—staff and professors included.

Everywhere you go, think about how you can leverage the relationships you develop, and not only with people you have classes with. Don't be afraid to step outside your little world and start shaking hands. Are there specific people you'd like to meet? Find out a little about them and what they like to do outside of the classroom. It's a lot easier to strike up a conversation with someone who's next to you on a charity walk than to hang around outside their office waiting for your chance. And do a little research into social events and what you have to do to get an invite. A lot of university presidents have open houses a few times a year that are open to students. Most students are too intimidated to go to these things, so these events are great networking opportunities.

Finally, join your school's alumni association and ask what you can do to help out. As a current student, you might be a great ambassador for your school. And be sure you make contact with the staff at the career center. Most of your fellow students wouldn't think of doing either of these things until after they've graduated—which just means more opportunities for you.

I know this may sound rather mercenary, and I'm not suggesting that you do anything insincere. But it doesn't hurt to keep this idea in the back of your mind when you're meeting people. And be sure to send a personal LinkedIn invite to everyone you connect with.

If You've Been out of Work Longer Than a Year

If you've been job searching for more than a year, make sure you have a strong story that explains what you've been doing besides sending out resumes. Did you take some courses, learn a language, travel extensively (especially to unusual locations), join the board of a not-for-profit, care for an elderly parent, get a PMP or FRM certification? It doesn't really matter what you did, just so long as you can speak intelligently and confidently about it. Otherwise, people may think that there's something wrong with you. Sad but true. It's still a pretty crappy market, but a lot of managers don't get that because they already have a job.

The point is to show that you're the kind of person who's always improving, who keeps current about industry trends, who's always moving forward.

If You've Been out of Work 10 Years or Longer

I often meet women (and some men) who have decided to come back into the workforce after raising kids. If this is true for you, spend some time thinking about all the things you did while you were out, and figuring out how to position them on your CV.

Leadership manifests itself in lots of different ways, from running events to fundraising to chairing a committee. Everything counts and you should include it all on your resume and LinkedIn profile.

At the same time, up-credentialing is critical, as is staying current on what's going on in your field. So if you're not already 100% up to date, read everything you can get your hands on, go to conferences (you'll probably be able to find some on YouTube), watch TED Talks, develop or brush up on your technical skills (again, start with YouTube), network with people in the field you want to be in, join trade associations and affinity groups as well as Toastmasters, which will help ensure that your presentation skills are outstanding for every possible interaction you might have with other people.

Think about taking courses on Coursera (coursera.org), Udemy (udemy.com), through one of the major universities (Harvard, Yale, UC Berkeley, Carnegie Mellon, and many others offer online classes), General Assembly (generalas semb.ly), or even through a local high school or community college.

Veterans

In today's job market, it's important to differentiate yourself from everyone else who's interviewing for the same job. And if you're just returning to civilian life after a stint (or an entire career) in the military, you're in a great position. You may have a little extra research to do, but the general mechanics of the job search are the same.

Companies that are run by vets—especially those that advertise that fact (Drexel Hamilton, for example)—are great places to start. So are companies that have special programs specifically created to attract veterans (VOWS: Veterans on Wall Street is just one of many), and those that don't have official programs but still want to assist former military personnel (such as JPMorgan and Goldman Sachs). And let's not forget about the many not-for-profits (like Wounded Warriors and Hire Heroes) that focus on helping veterans find jobs.

As a veteran—especially if you're retired—you may find some things about the civilian workplace more than a little frustrating. For example, a lot of organizations are either flat, or going flat. What I mean is that the hierarchical structure you were so used to during your military career—where seniority and experience generally translate into rank—is likely a thing of the past. You may report to someone substantially younger and more junior than you. But if he or she is running the project, you're going to have to gut it out (after all, no guts, no glory, right?). Oh, and resist the urge to call anyone Ma'am or Sir.

Speaking of resisting urges, you may want to avoid looking at your watch. In the military, you knew exactly when the workday started and you were never late. But in the civilian world, some of your co-workers may not share your punctuality. When people show up late (and they will), close your eyes and take a deep breath. You have no idea what their day, week, month, or life is like. Everyone has a crisis now and then, so try to be calm and be generous. There's so much in life that we have no control over, and one of those things is other people's lives. Don't bristle; don't remind them that they're late (chances are they already know that). Instead, smile, be gracious, and do yourself a favor: don't schedule your meetings so close together that someone else being late will make you late to your next event.

Chapter 12

Onboard or Overboard: Settling into Your New Job

Congratulations, You're Hired!

With the marketplace overflowing with highly qualified candidates who would love to have the job you just started, it's imperative that you fit in with the culture of the company, the team that's interviewing you, and the team you'll actually be working with. When Barbara began her new job at a not-for-profit, she brought the workplace habits and style that had made her a success on Wall Street. But what had worked so well in for-profit finance was a complete flop in a very different world. Three months later, Barbara was out looking for another job. And Chris, who is an aggressive extrovert, lasted only six weeks in what seemed like a dream job with a prestigious (and very conservative) investment bank.

Rule Number 1: "When in Rome…."

When you're trying to fit in with new people, a new job, and a new culture, if everyone wears slacks and a button-down shirt, you should too. If everyone wears a tie, wear one. If no one does, leave yours at home. (Generally speaking, it's a good idea to dress the same way your boss does.) Since this is your first time in Rome, it's understandable that you might need a little time to get the lay of the land, and to familiarize yourself with what, exactly, those Romans are doing. So if you show up on your first day at 8:30 a.m. and everyone else is already there, you'll want to get in at 8:00 or 8:15 the next morning. And if it looks like most people are staying after the time you thought the workday was ending, let your spouse or your babysitter know that you'll be a few minutes late. Over the course of a few weeks, you'll be able to align your schedule with the rest of your team, department, and firm.

Rule Number 2: Never Eat Alone.

Always ask someone to join you, even if you're just going down to the cafeteria to get a salad and bring it back to your desk. If everyone takes lunch at noon, you go with them. If they wait till 1:00, so do you. And don't wait to be asked out. If you see a bunch of folks about ready to head out, ask if you can join them. Try this with a few different groups of people.

Rule Number 3: Build Your Network.

At least twice a day—once in the morning and once in the afternoon—get out of your chair and do some walking around. You could be heading to the restroom, coffee room, or just checking out the floor. The purpose is to say hello to at least four people during that time and remember their names. Put names with faces and faces with departments; ask basic questions like what they've got planned for the weekend; and be sure to use people's names at least once every time you speak with them. Too many times seems a bit contrived. While you're doing your walkabouts, be sure to spend some time getting to know people in other departments. Bottom line: She who knows the most people and has the biggest network, wins—or at least keeps her job longer. When there are lay-offs and senior management has to pick between two people in similar roles, the one who has the most advocates in the room, the one more people know, is more likely to be spared. Knowledge, intelligence, and producing quality work aren't always enough.

Rule Number 4: Be a Real Part of the Team.

You may be new on the job, but that doesn't mean you can't mentor a younger or more junior member of your team. Puppies grow up to be dogs. Pete told me that the people who were most helpful to him in his job search were guys he had hired or mentored years before. If there's a holiday party, attend. If someone's collecting for a co-worker's birthday or new baby, contribute. If someone else's daughter is selling Girl Scout cookies or candy bars for charity, buy one. Sign every birthday card that makes the rounds and don't forget to show up in the conference room for cake.

Your ability to build alliances enterprise-wide in the first 90 days is critical to your long-term success. The people you work with and for must come to see you as part of the fabric of the organization. If they're looking for volunteers to help organize the company picnic, raise your hand. Believe me; they're just as curious to find out as much as they can about you as you are about them. Take the mystery out of it by showing up at typical after-work activities. If a few colleagues are going out for a drink, join them. Even if they're from a different department or floor. You can always leave after one beer or glass of wine, saying you have to head home. Remember, never get drunk or sloppy. This is why it's called work.

Rule Number 5: Be Yourself.

Whatever you do, be absolutely sure to stay true to who you really are. That's the guy (or gal) they hired—the one they like. So just keep on being the genuine you and you'll go far.

Under the guise of this recession, companies continue to release employees who don't fit in (of course, they're also getting rid of poor performers—but that's not you.) As I mentioned earlier, all things being equal, they'll retain the employee more people know and feel comfortable with.

Key Takeaways

- To fit in with new people, a new job, and a new culture, "When in Rome..."

- Never eat alone. Always ask someone to join you, even if you're just going down to the cafeteria to get a salad and bring it back to your desk.

- Build your network. At least twice a day—once in the morning and once in the afternoon—get out of your chair and do some walking around.

- You may be new on the job, but that doesn't mean you can't mentor a younger or more junior member of your team.

Notes

Frequently Asked Questions

1. **How long will it take me to get a job?**
   Count on 6–12 months working on it full-time—longer if you do it haphazardly.

2. **Will I make what I made last year?**
   Yes. Just ask. The market has improved a bit.

3. **Should I settle for less money/less title?**
   Generally speaking, no—unless you're switching industries or going into the not-for-profit sector instead of corporate. The one exception is if you're in dire need. If I were in that unfortunate situation, I'd wait tables if I had to. Check your budget and bank account.

4. **Should I go back more than 15 years in my resume?**
   Allocate most of the space to your accomplishments within the last 15 years. Put the rest in an Additional Work Experience section with less-detailed information—but only if the firms you worked for are household names or the functions and accomplishments you did were especially wonderful and truly add something to your resume. Leave out the dates and just put in the company, your title and responsibilities, and if appropriate, one accomplishment for at least the first one—especially if it's a big name.

5. **What if I want to change industries?**
   Think honestly about skills you've developed that you think would transfer well from your old industry to a new one.

Then meet with people who work in that industry and ask them whether your proposed move makes sense to them.

6. What do I do if I haven't been able to reach my target after three good tries (three emails, two emails and a phone call, and so on?)
   Call someone who has a relationship (personal and/or professional) with the person you're trying to reach, and ask what's going on with your target. Then call again. Chances are it's nothing personal, and it has nothing to do with you at all. If you still get nothing but silence, send an email saying, "So sorry we weren't able to connect this year. Be well."

7. How do I handle a panel interview?
   Maintain eye contact with the person asking the question but keep open body language for all—no arms crossed, smile, use all of their names. And sit up straight, face toward them, no slumping, no crossed arms.

8. How do I handle back-to-back (sequential) interviews?
   Be well-rested and prepared. Smile. Use everyone's name and be sure to make excellent eye contact with the person asking each question. Remember to breathe deeply, stand up, and stretch in between.

9. What do I say in the thank-you note?
   Thank them for their time, acknowledge something they talked about in the meeting, personalize the note, and ask about next steps. Always be deferential.

10. Should I send thank-you notes to everyone I met with in a panel interview? If so, how do I make those notes different—just in case they share them with each other?
    Yes, everyone gets a thank-you note. An email is fine, but a handwritten thank-you to the centers of influence/hiring managers might make sense and could be a tipping point and differentiator for you. Make sure the first sentence is the thank-you, the second sentence is about something they

talked about, and end with an actionable item—some kind of deliverable. For example, "Per our conversation, I will circle back to you by email late next week. I look forward to continuing our dialogue. Thanks again and best regards, Charlotte."

11. **What if I don't have a "dead mouse" to bring them?**
    Take the meeting anyway, but know if you're not giving, you may not get much in return. What goes around comes around. Try to give first, to get. Our society is built on the reciprocity principle. During the meeting, scope out ideas for dead mice in the future.

12. **Should I have a chronological or functional resume?**
    Chronological.

13. **How many references should I have?**
    Three to six, but don't include them on your resume. Be sure you've contacted them in advance and that you've given them talking points about you.

14. **Who pays when I have a networking meeting?**
    If you invited them, you pay. If they invited you, they pay. If anyone offers, let them. You're out of work and they know that. When they're out, it'll be your turn. You could also just leave the tip anytime or reach for your wallet and say, "Shall we split this?"

15. **How many networking meetings should I have each week?**
    Five to seven, face to face.

16. **What are the most important things to focus on in an interview?**
    What you're good at and how it will bring value to the organization you're interviewing with. Above all, always stay positive, ask strategic, good questions, use the interviewer's name, sit up straight (good posture depicts energy and attention), and smile. Remember that they should be doing most of the talking, not you.

17. **What are the most important things to focus on in a networking meeting?**

Be sure to bring your action plan with your complete list of target companies (you'll probably have 30–40 on your list). Then ask the person you're networking with whether he or she knows anyone at any of those companies, or whether he or she might be able to connect you with someone who does. Always be authentic. Build true rapport and ask what you can do for them.

18. **What else should I be doing?**

Keep (or stay) current by reading books and magazines that are relevant to your field, attending conferences, and meeting with people who are knowledgeable about the latest industry trends. Stay fit by going to the gym, walking, biking, swimming, or whatever makes you feel good and look great—employers like that. Get involved in volunteering and community work, so you look like you're compassionate and involved in the world around you.

For one free, personalized answer to your most
burning job-hunting question,
please visit Charlotte at
www.bringadeadmouse.com.

Author Biography

Charlotte A. Lee is a senior vice president, an executive coach, and the managing consultant for the New York and Stamford offices of Lee Hecht Harrison (LHH), the world's largest outplacement firm, with 300 offices in 67 countries. In this role, she is responsible for both coaching senior executives through career transition, and leading a team of more than a dozen colleagues. She coaches executives in a variety of industries, including financial services, consumer products, legal, telecom, media, and professional services. Additionally, Charlotte provides leadership-development coaching for senior executives currently in roles. In 2014, she was one of three recipients of the LHH Global Coach of the Year Award for "Exceptional Consulting/Coaching Performance." In 2014 and 2016, she was awarded the LHH SuperStar Award for being the number one coach in the Northeast.

Prior to LHH, Charlotte was the Lead Consultant of the New York office of DBM, where she led a team of coaches working with executives from global Fortune 1000 companies. Prior to DBM, she worked as a management consultant specializing in strategic planning, organizational development, and marketing, and was a career coach to senior executives. She has served as the Executive Director for five not-for-profits, including Habitat for Humanity, where she was the President for eight years. She currently serves on the Board of Directors of TruFund, Inc., and has been active with the National Kidney Foundation, having donated a kidney several years ago. An investment banker for more than 15 years, Charlotte worked at Credit Lyonnais Securities in Mergers and Acquisitions, in Corporate Finance at Alex. Brown, and at Kidder, Peabody & Co.

Ms. Lee has appeared on CNBC, Bloomberg Radio, and NPR, and has been interviewed by The Wall Street Journal, The New York Times, and Yahoo Finance. She was a panelist on the role of social media in career development for Fordham Law School and Ascend, the pan-Asian professional development association. She has presented on career development and leadership topics at many organizations, including GE, Deloitte, ING, RBC, State Street Bank, PwC, and the Financial Women's Association. Ms. Lee is the author of Bring a Dead Mouse: The Secret to Finding Your Perfect Job, which has garnered five stars on Amazon.

Charlotte is a certified literacy tutor and has taught conversational English to Chinese-Americans for many years. She has been active in the New York City public school system since 2002, as a Principal for a Day, part of the highly successful PENCIL program. In addition, she volunteers with Hire Heroes, a not-for-profit that assists veterans in getting civilian jobs. Charlotte holds a Bachelor of Arts from New York University and is certified in Leadership Effectiveness Analysis training. She lives in New York with her family.

Made in the USA
Middletown, DE
13 August 2019